Pro 4:7
Duane Vander Klok

SOLOMON SAYS:

Advice For Life From the Wisest Man Who Ever Lived

by Duane Vander Klok

ResLife Church
5100 Ivanrest Ave SW
Grandville, MI 49418

All scriptures NKJV unless otherwise stated.

Text formatting and design by Amy Cole, JPL Design Solutions

ISBN: 978-1-946671-04-2

Printed in the United States of America

CONTENTS

INTRODUCTION

Solomon was an amazing man! It is almost as if he won the greatest lottery of all time. Imagine this: when he was a newly appointed king, God granted Solomon one wish. Surprisingly, Solomon didn't respond as many would by asking for wealth or long life. Instead, Solomon asked God to give him the wisdom to rule God's people justly.

The Bible tells us that God was impressed with Solomon's response. He had unselfishly asked for God's help in fulfilling the task God had given him. So impressed was God with Solomon's response that He promised not only to grant the wish that Solomon had made, but most of the other wishes he could have wished as well! God gave Solomon the wisdom he requested plus wealth and power like nothing the world had ever seen.

According to the Bible, Solomon was the wisest man who had ever lived (until Jesus Christ arrived, of course). Since then, only Jesus has been wiser. 2 Chronicles 9 tells us, *"King Solomon was greater in riches and wisdom than all the other kings of the earth; all the kings of the earth sought audience with Solomon to hear the wisdom that God had put in his heart."*

Solomon was not only the wisest man alive, but the richest man alive, as well as the greatest achiever of his day. His success reached into nearly every arena. He had knowledge, wealth, and fame, as well as accomplishments both political and architectural. He became an incredible leader.

Just recently I was reading again in the book of Chronicles about how Solomon organized the nation of Israel and how he brought that nation to its absolute pinnacle during his reign. Since Solomon's time, never again has Israel returned to the height that it attained under his leadership.

With a fresh image in your mind of who Solomon is and what he accomplished, I want you to imagine that you are about to personally meet King Solomon, the richest and most powerful man in the world. You have entered his throne room which resembles the most beautiful museum you have ever seen. It is filled with one-of-a-kind items that Solomon received as gifts from the greatest leaders around the world. Never have you even dreamed of such exquisite surroundings.

After you have stopped in front of his throne, he leans forward a little and says, "I am glad you are here. I have thirty things that I want to say to you. These things are my favorites of all the wisdom nuggets God has given me. God Himself has asked me to pass them on to people of every generation. God Almighty attests that these truths will remain useful and applicable to every culture and every time, be it 1000 BC or 2018 AD."

After pausing and motioning to one of his many servants to bring you a desk with paper and pen, he continues. "These things that I will share with you can improve your marriage. They can revolutionize your finances. They can literally change your entire life. I would like to tell you what God wants you to know about your family, your money, your work, your gifts, skills, attitudes, friends, emotions, desires, and even your future. I want to teach you about judgment and prejudice, about the many things that will disappoint you, and what few things won't." Imagine that Solomon then looks you right in the eye and asks, "If I take the time to tell you these things, will you listen? Will you value them?"

I can hardly imagine that any of us would tell such an accomplished man, "No, thank you. I have something else I would rather do."

Although none of us living today have stood face to face with Solomon, he really did receive supernatural wisdom from God. More importantly for us, God really did ask him to pass it on. In fact, most of the chapters in the book of Proverbs are Solomon's way of passing the wisdom he received from God on to his son and all the following generations. There Solomon will tell us what he learned both when he chose to obey God and when he tried to find fulfillment outside of God.

Solomon says in Proverbs 22:20-21 (NIV), *"Have I not written thirty sayings for you, sayings of counsel and knowledge, teaching you true and reliable words, so that you can give sound answers to him who sent you?"* He's telling us that he has thirty things he wants us to be sure to hear. This book, *Solomon Says* is an exploration into this concise, but powerful, section of tips from Solomon on how we should live. Apart from Jesus Christ, Solomon was the most successful man that any of us are likely to be influenced by. I hope you will treat these thirty nuggets as timeless. They represent the wisdom that Solomon received directly from God.

Although I have tried to be thorough and helpful, there is, of course, much more that can be learned than I have time and space to include here. I encourage you not only to look at each chapter of this book for the information it holds, but also to watch for opportunities to delve deeper into each topic. You might call this Solomon's study guide for life. I am intentionally structuring the book to make it easy for you to use each topic as a separate springboard for discussion or study.

CHAPTER 1

INESCAPABLE JUSTICE

"Do not exploit the poor because they are poor and do not crush the needy in court, for the Lord will take up their case and will plunder those who plunder them."

Proverbs 22:22, NIV

A mother came to me in shock. "Is there no justice?" she cried, "How can that man get away with it?" She had just come from court where she was seeking justice for her 4-year old daughter who had been molested. Her daughter had described in detail what had happened to her but, because of her age, her testimony was not admissible in court. Without that information, the man was exonerated. Now the mother was in tears and completely unable to grasp how he could not be held accountable.

I felt frustrated and angry too, at this seeming lack of justice. Yet I was fully aware that God is neither unjust, nor was He unfaithful. I reminded her of this truth, saying, "He will be held accountable. There is a Judgment Day coming. God will take up your daughter's case. Although you may not see justice through the earthly court system, God will make 100% sure that there is justice."

God is a just God, and nothing is hidden from Him. Romans 12:19 reminds us that we do not need to avenge ourselves, but that we should leave room for God's wrath; *"For it is written, 'Vengeance is Mine, I will repay,'* says the Lord." There was only one thing the little girl's mother could do; forgive the man. As she did, she freed herself and her daughter from his sin and left him in God's hands to deal with.

We may feel angry and disappointed over the outcome of a case, but Solomon reminds us that earthly courts do not have the final say. Justice is not always served here and now by the courts of men. Although we might be treated wrongly and not see the justice we seek in the moment, there is a higher court and, though it be delayed, justice will always be served because God "will take up our case."

1 Timothy 5:24 says, *"Some men's sins are clearly evident, preceding them to judgment, but those of some men follow later."* In other words, some people get what is coming to them right away, but for others, it will follow them even beyond the grave. Solomon tells us to realize that we are not going to get away with anything. God is not mocked; whatever a man sows, that he will also reap (see Galatians 6:7).

A second theme in this nugget of wisdom is that we are not to exploit the poor or anyone over whom we may perceive ourselves superior. 1 Peter 1:17 (NIV) says, *"Since you call on a Father who judges each man's work impartially, live your lives as strangers here in reverent fear."*

Some of us may need reminding that God is not impressed with how smart we are. He's not impressed with our degrees, our titles, or positions. Neither is He impressed with our money. God is totally impartial in His judgment.

There are people who believe they are better than others because of their money, their education, their ethnicity, or even their skin color, but God disagrees. In Genesis 1:26, God said, *"Let Us make man in Our image, according to Our likeness; let them have dominion over the fish of the sea, over the birds of the air, and over the cattle, over all the earth…"* Notice that God gave us dominion over this earth and over the creatures of the earth; but God never gave man dominion over people. Anytime someone oppresses another human being based on a perceived difference, it is wrong. It doesn't matter if that difference is their economic status, their education, their appearance, or their ethnicity. Every time it happens, it is an abuse of authority. God said in Acts 17:26 that, *"He has made from one blood every nation of men."* In His eyes, every man and every woman has the same value. Jesus said a soul is worth more than the whole world. *"What will it profit a man,"* He asks, *"if he gains the world and loses his own soul?"* (Mark 8:36).

GOD NEVER GAVE MAN DOMINION OVER PEOPLE

Solomon begins his top thirty list by admonishing us to get our heads out of the sand and begin viewing each other the way God does. In God's eyes, no one has "preferred" status. Nothing escapes God's ultimate judgment. God will take up the cause of the poor and disadvantaged.

In the book of Esther, Haman was the assistant to the king who thought he was "all that and a bag of chips." He believed that his riches, his title, his position, and even his ethnicity gave him the right to oppress the Jewish people. He constructed gallows on which to hang Mordecai the Jew, a man who refused to honor him. In addition, he arranged for the slaughter of all the Jews in the entire kingdom. For a while, it looked as if he would succeed.

Suddenly, God turned the tables on him. In a bold act that could have cost Queen Esther her life, she exposed his corruption, and in one day Haman lost all his riches. His prestige and position were given to Mordecai, the very person he most wanted to oppress. In addition, by the end of the day it was Haman's body that was swinging from the 75-foot-high gallows that he had built for Mordecai to hang on.

Justice does not always come to a person so quickly. Many times it may appear that crimes go unnoticed and that some people are above reproach, but the wise realize that God sees, God cares, He is just, and He is not mocked. Every story will end with justice being served—sometimes the ending is just further down the road than we expected.

> *"Commit your way to the Lord, trust also in Him, and He shall bring it to pass. He shall bring forth your righteousness as the light, and your justice as the noonday."* (Psalm 37:5, 6)

If you realize that you have wronged others, know this: God, who is just, loves each of us so much that He laid the burden of all our wrongdoing on Jesus Christ. Jesus took our guilt that we might be justified through Him. We can receive His gift of having justice served to Him in our place—or we can reject His gift of forgiveness and receive the justice we deserve. *"If we confess our sins, He is faithful and just to forgive us our sins and to cleanse us from all unrighteousness"* (1 John 1:9).

CHAPTER 2

THE DANGER OF ANGER

"Do not make friends with a hot-tempered man, do not associate with one easily angered, or you may learn his ways and get yourself ensnared."

Proverbs 22:24-25, NIV

This is a very different warning from those you may have received if you grew up focused on finding the "right crowd." Solomon is <u>not saying</u> to associate only with people of like social status. He's not urging you to make sure that everyone around you makes you feel comfortable, and he's not saying to have friends who are a step up rather than down the social ladder from you so they will pull you up, not down. What Solomon is talking about here is character. It is character, not income, which makes a difference. It is character, not similarity of culture, which makes a good friend. Moreover, Solomon has focused on one particular character flaw as being perhaps the most dangerous. Let's look at another statement made by Solomon: *"Do not hasten in your spirit to be angry, for anger rests in the bosom of fools"* (Ecclesiastes 7:9).

Maybe you thought "road rage" was a new thing; that it is the stress of a technological age that causes otherwise peaceful people to become angry. However, Solomon wrote these words long before traffic jams, time clocks, and credit card bills! Anger has been making fools of people for centuries. You know the ones Solomon is talking about. You see them walking through the mall or driving down the road with a smile on their face. Yet as soon as the littlest thing goes wrong, they absolutely explode! The truth is, they didn't get mad that fast; they were already mad. They are walking around mad 24/7, 365 days a year. The Bible says that their anger "rests in their bosom." That means it is right there under the surface—ready to explode at any time.

Listen to Solomon's divinely inspired advice about these people. He says, *"When you find someone like that, do not associate with that person for it will become a snare to you; you will learn to be like them"* (paraphrase of Proverbs 22:24-25). When you find someone whose anger is just under the surface, it is unresolved conflict every time. Somewhere, back down the line, they believe somebody mistreated them and they have not forgiven them. Because they have not dealt with their anger, it constantly simmers under the surface.

Anger itself is not wrong. In fact, you can even be angry without sinning. Basically, anger is a strong feeling of exasperation or dislike over something. Everyone feels it from time to time. It is one of the many feelings we are all wired with. But that doesn't give us an excuse to act ugly or do wrong to others! Instead, we should think of anger as an alarm to tell us that we need to deal with something.

It is our responsibility to choose to deal with anger the right way. Ephesians 4:26 says, *"'Be angry, and do not sin': do not let the sun go down on your wrath, nor give place to the devil."* If held in the heart, anger fuels unforgiveness, inspires resentment, and breeds bitterness. It leads to unkind words and actions that cause damaging wounds and great regret. Bitterness poisons the person holding it and ruins even the best of their relationships.

The truth is, we should not even end our prayers with "amen" if we have anger in our hearts! Jesus said, *"And whenever you stand praying, if you have anything against anyone, forgive him, that your Father in heaven may also forgive you your trespasses"* (Mark 11:25). Forgiving is something you are to do when you pray, or literally, "whenever you pray." Some translations even say "every time you pray." I believe Jesus said that expecting us to pray at least once every day! We are to go to God with the issues that angered us, receive His grace to forgive those who hurt us, and leave them in God's hands.

"Don't let the sun go down on your wrath," we are told. You were not designed to stay angry. You need to release it and to forgive. If you do not, you will become one of those people with a smile on their face but with anger resting just under the surface. And, from time to time, explosions will occur!

Nobody goes to the doctor and says, "I accidentally touched a hot stove yesterday and it hurt for several seconds. Can you make sure I never feel any pain again?" However, if you twist your knee on Monday, and it is still just as painful 24 hours later, you would likely say, "There is something very wrong." You would try to find out how to get rid of the pain. The brief pain from a hot stove is informative and helpful, but continuous pain is just plain miserable. Some things are not meant to last more than a short while. Anger is one of those things.

"See to it that no one falls from God's grace; that no bitterness springs up to cause trouble and spoil everybody's life" Hebrews 12:15 (TNT). The Bible says that if you are that person that has anger resting in your bosom, "it will spring up." Notice what it says will happen next: "it will spoil everybody's life." It doesn't just spoil your life, or even the life of the one who you are mad at. Instead, it will spoil your spouse's life, and it will spoil

SOME THINGS ARE NOT MEANT TO LAST MORE THAN A SHORT WHILE. ANGER IS ONE OF THOSE THINGS.

your child's life. It will spoil your co-workers life. Everybody around you will be affected because bitterness and hatred cannot be focused like a laser beam; they are always like atomic bombs leaving collateral damage in every direction.

That is why the Bible tells us to watch our associations. In Proverbs 14:29 (NIV), Solomon says, "*A patient man has great understanding, but a quick-tempered man displays folly.*" Proverbs 19:19 (NIV) says, "*A hot-tempered man must pay the penalty; if you rescue him, you will have to do it again.*" Why will he repeat the same mistake? It is because he has anger resting in his bosom, and no matter how hard he tries to keep a smile on his face, he can't. Because he refuses to release his anger by forgiving, he cannot help but blow up again and again.

We also cannot afford to forget the last part of Mark 11:25 where we are instructed to forgive so our Father in heaven may also forgive us our trespasses. When you forgive, the anger that has been resting in your bosom will begin to dissolve, and you literally become a different person.

Jesus says your heart needs to be searched for unresolved conflict and unforgiveness regularly. At the least, each time you pray. You shouldn't go to sleep or say "amen" while still reserving the right to stay angry with anyone. If you are interested in living life to the fullest, you must learn to release your anger daily. You must develop the habit of forgiveness and make patience a way of life.

Remember, the character of those with whom you choose to associate will make a huge impact on the quality and direction of your life. An angry, short-tempered person is damaging to anyone foolish enough to stay close. Proverbs 13:20 (NIV) says, "*He who walks with the wise grows wise, but the companion of fools suffers harm.*" In the New Testament, 1 Corinthians 15:33 (NIV) reinforces this saying, "*Do not be misled: Bad company corrupts good character.*"

CHAPTER 3

CO-SIGNING & GAMBLING

"Do not be a man who strikes hands in pledge or puts up security for debts; if you lack the means to pay, your very bed will be snatched from under you."

Proverbs 22:26-27

In today's language, we would call "putting up security" co-signing. This verse is telling you not to be a cosigner, because it can come back to sting you when and where you least expect it. This is particularly interesting when you consider that this comes from Solomon, the richest man in the world.

This reminds me of what my friend and fellow pastor, Jimmy Evans, says about his father-in-law. His father-in-law is a very wealthy man, worth hundreds of millions of dollars, but Jimmy says, "You know, he's the most teachable person I've ever met when it comes to money. He's always studying and going to seminars. He hires the best people he can find to give him advice concerning his finances."

Often, the wealthiest individuals are the most cautious and teachable concerning their finances. Then there are those of us who really need every advantage we can get, but instead of sounding like Solomon or Jimmy Evans' father-in-law, we say, "I know what I want to do. It's what I've always done, and I don't want to hear anybody telling me anything to the contrary." The truth is, if we want financial success we need to be willing to be teachable.

Solomon desires to teach us that it is unwise to "be surety" or to cosign. I have personally made several people upset by following this advice. In fact, several years ago a staff member of mine became visibly angry with me when I said that I would not cosign. The ironic thing was this: the staff member was looking for help because someone he had cosigned for did not make their payments. This left the staff member legally responsible, and he was forced to pay. Now, there he was, mad at me because I would not do the very thing that got him into trouble.

In Proverbs 6:1-5 (NIV), Solomon talks again about co-signing. If you have done it for someone, his advice is this: *"Do this, my son, to free yourself, since you have fallen into your neighbor's hands. Go and humble yourself; press your plea with your neighbor! Allow no sleep to your eyes, no slumber to your eyelids. Free yourself, like a gazelle from the hand of the hunter, like a bird from the snare of the fowler."* That is pretty clear. You should avoid co-signing like the plague.

Perhaps you are thinking, "Ok I get it, don't do it. But I don't really understand what is so bad about it." The reason cosigning is so dangerous is that it perverts a spiritual principle. Here is the concept Solomon is trying to show us: "Authority and responsibility go hand in hand." In other words, you should never seek to be responsible for something over which you do not have authority.

AUTHORITY AND RESPONSIBILITY GO HAND IN HAND.

Consider what takes place when you cosign for someone. You literally and legally accept responsibility for their debt without being given any authority over how they handle their finances. That is a perversion of a spiritual principle.

I remember hearing a story about a man in the seventies who organized a large teaching crusade. He rented a ballroom, did some advertising, and invited several of the nation's top Bible teachers to come. It was to be a huge Bible teaching seminar. If I recall correctly, the budget for the meeting was about $25,000. There were going to be meetings on Thursday night, Friday morning, Friday afternoon, Friday night, and Saturday.

On the first night, the organizer received an offering to go toward the meeting's expenses. After the meeting, a random attendee came up to the man organizing the event and said, "The Lord just spoke to me and told me that you are not supposed to take any more offerings and that all of the bills are going to be paid." The meeting organizer gave a response that I believe was divinely inspired. He said, "That's great! If you will sign to pay for anything that doesn't come in, I won't take any more offerings." The would-be prophet said, "Well no, I'm not going to be responsible for anything; I'm just telling you what you should do." That man wanted authority without having any responsibility.

Remember this: whenever there is responsibility, there also needs to be authority. Wherever you find responsibility with no authority, it is a perversion, and that is what is happening when you cosign for someone else. You are accepting equal responsibility for their debt without having any authority to ensure that they will pay. The Bible says, "Do not do it!"

The only exception to this rule is if you would joyfully *give* the person the money to pay for it. In other words, if someone asks you to cosign and you know, should a scenario arise where they are unable to make their payments, that you would be happy to pay their bill in full for them with no strings attached, then I *might* say go ahead. Just do not trick yourself; you need to be fully and un-begrudgingly willing and able to give them with no promise of repayment every penny that you are taking responsibility for. There is a good chance you may have to do just that.

CHAPTER 4

STEALING

"Do not steal your neighbor's property by moving the ancient boundary markers set up by your ancestors."
Proverbs 22:28, NLT

This is pretty straight-forward: do not take what doesn't belong to you. It is safe to say that most of us aren't likely to walk into our neighbor's home with a gun and take their belongings. However, notice Solomon mentioned that even acquiring a little extra land by moving the surveyor's stake is wrong. Our culture tempts us to view things, not so much in terms of what is right and wrong, but in terms of what is hurtful and not hurtful.

Here are some questions to help illustrate this point:

Which is a greater sin?

a.) Taking money from someone whose need is so great that they will definitely notice it is gone.

b.) Taking money from someone who has so much that they will never realize it is missing.

If you thought to yourself, "Stealing from the poor is worse than stealing from the rich," then your standard is cultural not Biblical. I hope you realize that both acts are equally sinful. Solomon is saying you should not steal—even if no one is likely to notice or if no one will be hurt by it.

Here is another question. Which is worse:

a.) Stealing $1,000,000?

b.) Stealing $2,000,000?

Does the size of what is stolen make the act more wrong? If it is the heart and not the dollar amount that matters, then how does God view stealing a ten dollar stapler from the office? Did you ever consider that Adam and Eve's sin involved just a small piece of fruit? Maybe there aren't any bank robbers reading this book, but it is a safe assumption that many of us still struggle with the desire to take what isn't ours, especially when we think it might never be noticed or missed. So what are we to do?

Ephesians 4:28 says, *"Let him who stole steal no longer, but rather let him labor, working with his hands what is good, that he may have something to give him who has need."* Perhaps the most powerful words of this verse are at the end: "to give." It DOES NOT say that thieves should learn to work for what *they want.* What it DOES say is that thieves need to learn how to work for something *to give.*

The key to living a life free from the desire to take what isn't ours, lies in discovering the joy of giving. Jesus said, *"It is more blessed to give than to receive"* (Acts 20:35). Employees who go to work each day with the mindset that they are there to get as much for themselves as they can will be takers. They will take longer breaks,

THE KEY TO LIVING A LIFE FREE FROM THE DESIRE TO TAKE WHAT ISN'T OURS, LIES IN DISCOVERING THE JOY OF GIVING.

they will spend work time taking personal calls, they will leave early, and office supplies will go home with them. Psychologists tell us these people don't even consider what they are doing as stealing. They rationalize that, since the purpose of work is to benefit them, they deserve these things. So they do the minimum of what is required to receive the financial compensation they came for, and they often feel entitled to a little more.

Contrast that with workers having a Biblical understanding. They realize that it is more blessed to give than to receive. They enjoy blessing their employer and customers with their very best. They don't mind answering the phone one last time—even after they have punched out—because they aren't plagued with the feeling that they are owed more than they might receive. They have discovered the joy of giving! For them, another spiritual law has kicked in: "*Give, and it will be given to you: good measure, pressed down, shaken together, and running over*" (Luke 6:38).

Who do you think has the best job security when times get tough? Who is the most likely to be given a promotion? Without a doubt it is the giver. When giving becomes a lifestyle, the temptation to take what isn't yours disappears. Solomon said this about things acquired dishonestly "*Bread gained by deceit is sweet to a man, but afterward his mouth will be filled with gravel*" (Proverbs 20:17). This means that the satisfaction you expect to receive from stealing your employer's time or money will elude you. It will be like trying to catch your shadow; it will never feel like enough, and it will never satisfy you. Even after taking extra breaks, instead of feeling satisfied that you got what you deserved, you will still feel entitled to more.

> "*The world of the generous gets larger and larger; the world of the stingy gets smaller and smaller.*"
> (Proverbs 11:24 The Message)

When we give, our world and our influence becomes larger. Our hearts also become larger as our concern for others enlarges our hearts. The world of the stingy gets smaller and smaller as their only concern is for themselves. If we follow Solomon's advice we will discover the joy and fulfillment God desires for us. No one can take enough time, money, or other "valuables" to become truly satisfied. But, those who live to give discover that blessing others actually blesses them the most.

CHAPTER 5

DEVELOPING SKILLS AND TALENTS

"Do you see a man who excels in his work? He will stand before kings; he will not stand before unknown men."

Proverbs 22:29

Many of us have been trained to think that a job is about what we get. For this reason, statisticians tell us that most people today—over half—are not satisfied with their jobs. You see, they *decided* what to do instead of *discovering* what they are supposed to do. A decision based on how I can get what I need isn't God's idea of career placement. He wants us to discover what He has gifted us with that we can give to others. The Bible says, "*Train up a child in the way he should go...*" (Proverbs 22:6). The Amplified version says it this way:

"Train up a child in the way he should go [and in keeping with his individual gift or bent]..."

Every one of us has a gift from God. The Bible speaks again of that gift in Proverbs 18:16 which says, *"A man's gift makes room for him and brings him before great men."*

See a man who works hard →

That gift always starts out in seed form. It is a small thing. It is a bent toward a certain something that needs to grow and to be developed. That gift is what God designed to carry you in life. It can bring you before great men; some translations say it can even bring you before kings.

In life, you are rewarded by how helpful you are, not by how selfish you are. You are rewarded for the problems you solve and how well you solve them. This week, my bicycle broke so I had to take it and have some work done on it. I think it cost me about $37.50 for each hour the mechanic worked on it. However, if I have to call a lawyer, it is much more expensive. A lawyer will charge me more like $350 dollars an hour. I thank God that I do not need brain surgery, but for those who do, it costs somewhere around $12,000 dollars an hour.

IN LIFE, YOU ARE REWARDED BY HOW HELPFUL YOU ARE, NOT BY HOW SELFISH YOU ARE.

What is the difference between these workers? They solve different problems and they are rewarded for the problems they solve. If you say, "I am not making enough money," the answer will boil down to this: you either need to solve different problems or do a better job with the ones you currently solve.

When David fought and defeated the giant he was rewarded with a large financial compensation, a lifelong tax exemption, and he was supposed to marry the king's daughter. You might ask, "Well, why was the pay so high for just going out for a few minutes to fight Goliath?" The answer, of course, is that nobody else could do it. He solved a problem that nobody else could.

God has gifted every person with something. Each of us needs to discover what our gift is, and then we need to sharpen that gift. Make it your life's pursuit to keep improving the gift God has given you.

I like very much what Martin Luther King Jr. said. "If it falls your lot to be a street sweeper, sweep streets like Michelangelo painted pictures, like Shakespeare wrote poetry, like Beethoven composed music. Sweep streets so well that all the host of Heaven and Earth will have to pause and say, 'Here lived a great street sweeper, who swept his job well.'" It's your gift; it will make room for you. Sometimes it may be a natural gift, but it is still something God gives you. He always seems to give us our gifts in seed form. No matter how developed you feel your gift is, you can always develop it further through good stewardship.

Today I pastor a church and even write books but it didn't start like this. Just over 40 years ago, Jeanie and I were living in Dallas while I was finishing Bible school. Jeanie had a job cleaning houses in the afternoon for a little extra money. I would drive her to the home where she needed to clean, and I would spend the time studying. At one particular home, the couple had a son who was thirteen or fourteen years old. They asked me, "Could you do a Bible study with him? He could really use something like that." I agreed to do it, and that first week I led a Bible study for one person. The next week he invited a friend, and my "congregation" grew by 100%! The third week, the friend's mother also came—most likely to make sure that I wasn't teaching heresy. That week, I had 50% growth. My point is simply this: start where you are today. Take what God has given you, and although it is in seed form, develop it, sharpen it, and it will grow.

I remember sitting in a car many years ago with Lester Sumerall. He was trying to impress the importance of learning on Jeanie and me. He said, "If you graduate today, and you learn nothing tomorrow, you are already behind. Keep on learning and keep on growing." That truth applies both to your spiritual life and to the gift, skill, or craft that God has given you.

Multimillionaire Peter Daniels said, "The average American spends less than $10 per year to improve their skill, their call, or their business." If that statistic is anywhere close to the truth, what a shame! We need to be intentional about not allowing ourselves to become comfortable where we are. We need to nurture the desire to keep growing.

Have you ever noticed that often times, instead of us preparing for the next step and then taking it intentionally, our circumstances almost have to force us to grow? When we first entered full-time ministry, we moved to Mexico with a plan to assist a missionary who already had an established church. After we had been there only six weeks the missionary came to me saying, "We are packing our stuff and we are leaving." Anticipating that he had a plan, I asked, "What about the church?"

He responded, "Well, we are leaving, here are the keys; you can have it." In my shock, I blurted out, "But, I don't want it." To my surprise, he just said, "If you don't want it, just stay home and let the devil have it. We are leaving!"

So that was my first promotion. The very next night I was preaching. We had only been in the country six weeks, and I still spoke almost no Spanish. To be honest, I was very grateful that I had to speak through an interpreter because that gave me extra time after each sentence to come up with what I was going to say next! I hoped it looked like I was just pausing for him to translate.

I preached that way for seven months, and then one night I arrived at church ready to speak. I looked around and didn't see my interpreter anywhere. When I asked where he was, someone finally answered that he had been in a motorcycle accident with a bus and that he was in the hospital. Naturally, I asked, "Who is going to translate?" They said, "Nobody." So once again I was forced to grow.

That was my first sermon in Spanish, and my wife Jeanie can attest to what happened. I was actually doing pretty well until the altar call. I was supposed to tell the people they could find forgiveness for their "pecados" which is the Spanish word for "sin," instead I said "pescados" which means "fish." Oh my!

The following week, I was talking about the blood of Jesus. I wanted to say, "Jesus was a special man," which should have come out as, "Un Hombre especial." Instead I said, "Un Hombre espacial," which means a space-man or astronaut. All through the sermon, I kept referring to Jesus, the astronaut, and I couldn't figure out why everybody was laughing and smiling.

In Exodus 36:1 (NIV), it says, *"So Bezalel, Oholiab, and every skilled person to whom the Lord has given skill and ability to know how to carry out all the work of constructing the sanctuary are to do the work just as the Lord has commanded."* I want to point out here that this verse disproves a mindset that many Christians have. God doesn't just anoint people for spiritual or ministerial roles. Here, God had anointed people to do construction work. God can anoint you to run a business or to get sales. God's anointing and his gifting can be on us for an infinite variety of jobs. He gives the gifts, and he desires that we would take them, grow them and develop them for His glory.

CHAPTER 6

SELF-CONTROL

"When you sit down to eat with a ruler, consider carefully what is before you; and put a knife to your throat if you are a man given to appetite. Do not desire his delicacies, for they are deceptive food."

Proverbs 23:1-3

The application of what Solomon is telling us here goes beyond just the food that we eat. He is talking about self-control and balance. While he did say, of course, that we shouldn't allow our appetites to get out of control, the issue of self-control extends to nearly every area of our lives. It includes, but is not limited to, food, money, and sex.

There is an important lesson to be found here.

SOMETHING DOES NOT NEED TO BE INHERENTLY BAD IN ORDER TO BE DAMAGING.

Something does not need to be inherently bad in order to be damaging. Satan, the Bible tells us, "...*comes only to steal and kill and destroy*" (from John 10:10, NIV). He is just as content to destroy by misusing something that is good and necessary as he is to use something that has no redeeming value.

We would easily agree that we need food every day, yet gluttony is wrong. We all know money is necessary for our daily lives, but the Bible says, *"the love of money is the root of all evil."* (1 Timothy 6:10) Sex inside the confines of marriage is a wonderful blessing designed by God. However, outside of the marriage covenant, it is sinful and not a blessing. Satan will always try to take something God has given you as a blessing and convince you to abandon self-control in that area. Remember this: sin always takes you farther than you thought you'd ever go, it always keeps you longer than you ever thought you'd stay, and it will cost you more than you ever thought you'd pay. Always!

SIN ALWAYS TAKES YOU FARTHER THAN YOU THOUGHT YOU'D EVER GO, IT ALWAYS KEEPS YOU LONGER THAN YOU EVER THOUGHT YOU'D STAY, AND IT WILL COST YOU MORE THAN YOU EVER THOUGHT YOU'D PAY. ALWAYS!

Every mile of road has 2 miles of ditch.

It is good to keep in mind that the devil doesn't care which "ditch" you are in, just as long as you aren't on the road where you belong. If he cannot keep you out of church, then he will try to convince you that you have to earn salvation through good works. He will take something good and try to make it into an unhealthy obsession. He wants to see you abuse every blessing you have.

That is why we need self-control. Yes, I am telling you that you will face temptation, but I am also telling you that there is no temptation you will ever face that cannot be conquered. Don't just take my word for it though. 1 Corinthians 10:13 says, *"No temptation has overtaken you except such as is common to man."* This means that whatever vice or imbalance tempts you, it is not a VIP temptation. You may think, "Nobody has ever been tempted like this. Nobody has ever felt quite what I feel. Nobody has ever had this desire or such a strong pull. I am certain no one can fully understand my situation."

The moment that thought enters your head, you should immediately recognize where it came from: Satan has been trying that lie for years! Millions have felt all the pull and pressure of temptation that you have and been tempted in the same way. All of our temptations are common to man. This is where the second part of 1 Corinthians 10:13 comes into play. It says, *"…but God is faithful, who will not allow you to be tempted beyond what you are able, but with the temptation will also make the way of escape, that you may be able to bear it."* This is the truth.

When temptation comes, God has already measured that temptation and measured you—and He has concluded that you are able to come through it victoriously. Comedian Flip Wilson may have said, "The Devil made me do it," but that is not reality. The devil cannot make you do anything, because God has guaranteed that there is always a way of escape and that you can bear it. So remember when you are facing an extra difficult temptation, God has promised a way of escape for you.

Solomon talked about temptation because he knew it was important. He knew that you would need to know the truth about your tempting situations. Jesus said, *"If you abide in My word, you are My disciples indeed. And you shall know the truth, and the truth shall make you free."* (John 8:31,32). That is why, when Jesus was tempted by the devil, He responded again and again saying, *"It is written"* (see Luke 4:1-13). Jesus fought temptation with truth, and so should we.

"What is the truth?" you may ask. The truth is that this temptation isn't anything special or insurmountable. The truth is that God has guaranteed you a way out. One of those ways out includes prayer.

2 Timothy 2:26 says to pray *"that they may come to their senses and escape the snare of the devil having been taken captive by him to do his will; pray that God will grant them repentance."*

If there is a sin that seems to have you caught you should pray that God will grant you repentance. Much of the power of temptation is broken when we see the consequences that sin will bring. Pray that God will grant you the wisdom to see how that sin will hurt you and those you love. Pray that God reminds you of your commitment to Him and gives you His strength at the very moment you need it.

CHAPTER 7

KEEP MONEY IN PROPER PERSPECTIVE

"Do not overwork to be rich; Because of your own understanding, cease! Will you set your eyes on that which is not? For riches certainly make themselves wings; they fly away like an eagle toward heaven."

Proverbs 23:4-5

There are many situations we face that only money can solve. The electric company, for example, doesn't ask for your prayers; they want your money. One way or another, it requires money to keep the lights on at your house. Have you ever noticed, however, that many people expect money will do more for them than just pay bills? Some expect money to make them happy. Others expect that money will solve their relationship problems or provide them with a sense of significance.

Solomon knows what he is talking about when he discusses money. Remember, he was perhaps the richest man that ever lived. In his hometown there was so much gold that silver wasn't even considered of value. (1 Kings 10:21). Let's listen again to what Solomon said in Proverbs 23:4-5, this time from the New International Version of the Bible:

> *"Do not wear yourself out to get rich; have the wisdom to show restraint. Cast but a glance at riches, and they are gone, for they will surely sprout wings and fly off to the sky like an eagle."*

Solomon through divine inspiration says, "Have the wisdom to show restraint." In other words, he is saying, "If you are smart, you won't pursue money as if that is all that matters."

Isaiah 55:2 asks and answers an important question: *"Why do you spend money for what is not bread, and your wages for what does not satisfy? Listen carefully to Me, and eat what is good, and let your soul delight itself in abundance."* Notice the same theme? The things money can buy cannot satisfy you; money is temporary.

My favorite translation of Psalms 49 is the New Jerusalem Bible. Starting in verse 17, it says, *"When he dies, the rich man will take nothing with him; his wealth will not go down with him."* The only place you and I get to use our money is here on earth. No matter how many funeral processions you've seen, I am certain that you have never seen a hearse pulling a U-Haul trailer!

Earlier in that Psalm we are told, *"No one can ever redeem himself or pay his own ransom to God, the price for himself is too high; it can never be that he will live on forever and avoid the sight of the abyss"* (Psalms 49:7 NJB). Money cannot redeem you. No matter how much you give, it will never buy your salvation. The Bible reiterates this in 1 Peter 1:18-19, where it says, *"You were not redeemed with corruptible things, like silver or gold, from your aimless conduct received by tradition from your fathers, but with the precious blood of Christ."*

My favorite part of Psalm 49 is in verses 12&13. It observes, *"In prosperity, people lose their good sense, they become no better than dumb animals. So they go on in their self-assurance, right up to the end, they are content with their lot. (NJB)"* Did you notice the warning that prosperity can cause you to lose good sense? Money can cause you to think that you are permanently set and provided for when, in fact, you are not.

Psalm 49 continues, *"Though he pampered himself while he lived—and people praise you for looking after yourself—he will go to join the ranks of his ancestors, who will never again see the light"* (Psalm 49:18-19, NJB)

The Bible is warning us not to be lulled into googly-eyed admiration of the rich. Don't assume that, just because someone has money to pamper themselves here and now, they truly are deserving of envy. No matter how many people, magazines, or television programs exalt the rich as admirable, enviable, and worthy of emulation simply because of their wealth, in God's eyes, they are still fools if eternity is not their first priority. What is the eternal? It is our relationship with God and the well-being of our souls.

We can never accurately say that money is of no value to us. Obviously, there are many things for which money is needed. It is interesting that Solomon balances his comments on money by stating in Ecclesiastes 10:19: *"Money is the answer for everything."* The key phrase to understanding his statement is "under the sun." Twenty six times throughout the book of Ecclesiastes, Solomon reminds us that he is talking about only the things "under the sun." There is no denying that money is useful in certain situations but for the things that really matter, the things that really last, money is useless.

There is one way in particular that money relates to true riches. Luke 16:11 says *"Therefore if you've not been faithful in the unrighteous mammon, who will commit to your trust the true riches?"* God says although you cannot buy true riches with money, what you do with your money is a test by which your ability to handle true riches will be revealed. Take a moment to consider what that says about America. Statistically, that means a lot of people in our culture are very undeserving of true riches.

Remember, Solomon said, *"Cast but a glance at riches, and they are gone, for they will surely sprout wings and fly off to the sky like an eagle"* (Proverbs 23:4-5, NIV). There are so many ways to lose money that are out of your control. You can lose money in a fire or it can fly away in a financial collapse, a lawsuit, a robbery, and the list goes on. But the things that money cannot buy, such as peace, joy, a right relationship with God, a strong family, and others, cannot be taken away unless you let them go.

When Satan attacked Job, the very first thing he attacked was Job's finances, but that doesn't mean God doesn't care about our money. 3 John 2:2 says: *"Beloved, I pray that you may prosper in all things and be in health, just as your soul prospers."* God desires financial blessing for you.

Sometimes you can believe something that is untrue, and it really doesn't matter; other times, it could literally cost you everything. For example, if you believe the moon is made of blue cheese and that Santa Claus is real, what difference does it make? Your understanding of the chemical composition of the moon doesn't affect your daily life at all. On the other hand, if you are about to cross the street and don't believe there is a car coming, but there really is, that could drastically affect you!

In regards to money, many of the untruths we believe cause major problems in our lives. Statistics tell us that up to 75% of all divorces are attributed to financial difficulty. There are men and women in prison because they did something illegal to get money. There are husbands neglecting their families because they have become workaholics in pursuit of the almighty dollar. Many young people are devastated because a lack of money prevents them from going to college and getting a good education.

IN REGARDS TO MONEY, MANY OF THE UNTRUTHS WE BELIEVE CAUSE MAJOR PROBLEMS IN OUR LIVES.

How you interact with money will undoubtedly have a serious effect on your life. That's why you should place a very high priority

on identifying any beliefs you have about money that are not biblical. When it comes to money, what you believe is very important,
and what you don't know about it can and does affect you.

- Money can't give you significance.

- Money can't give you a great marriage.

- Money can't make you 100% safe.

- Money can't guarantee your health.

Don't wear yourself out pursing money, believing it will fulfill
your life.

CHAPTER 8

UNITY AND THE POWER OF SYNERGY

"Do not eat the food of a stingy man, do not crave his delicacies; for he is the kind of man who is always thinking about the cost. "Eat and drink," he says to you, but his heart is not with you. You will vomit up the little you have eaten and will have wasted your compliments."

Proverbs 23:6-8 (NIV)

What nugget from this passage did Solomon feel was worthy of inclusion in his "top thirty"? It is the importance of unity. Let's take a moment to discuss this example of someone who says they want you to enjoy yourself, but in reality, their heart is not for you at all.

Unity is more than just agreement; it is actually a spiritual force. The Bible says, *"One chases a thousand but two can chase ten thousand"* (Deuteronomy 32:30). Wait a minute: the math we learned in first grade would have us believe that if one person can chase 1,000, then two can chase 2,000; yet, the scripture said two could chase 10,000! The term for this inexplicable multiplication of efficiency is "synergy."

Synergy, one of God's special surprises, means that the whole is greater than the sum of its parts. We see it in the physical world when two oxen yoked together can pull far more than the combined weight of what each could pull alone.

There is a story about an ox pulling contest in Canada. The first place ox pulled 8,000 pounds and the second place ox pulled just a little less than that. The two ox were yoked together. Simple math would have us expect that they could pull around 16,000 pounds combined. When they actually put the two oxen in front of the weights, the two of them pulled over 26,000 pounds!

Synergy is every bit as real in the spiritual realm when two or more pray in agreement or when a husband and wife chose to be united. The benefits in both situations far exceed what either of them could have cumulatively accomplished alone.

Unity is spiritual, and we are all spiritual beings. Even if you are not accustomed to noticing the spiritual side of situations, that doesn't mean they aren't there. Have you ever experienced a time where a group of people all claimed to be in agreement, but you somehow knew it really wasn't so? Perhaps it was a conversation with your spouse or maybe a meeting at work where everyone was nodding their heads saying, "I agree, I agree." You saw and heard what they were saying but your spirit recognized there was no spiritual synergy and that the agreement was insincere.

As Solomon was trying to tell us, insincere words are a cheap substitute for true unity. True unity is at an attitude level. In fact, in the Kingdom of God attitude is everything. In 1 Corinthians 9:17 the Apostle Paul says this: "*If I preach voluntarily, I have a reward; if not voluntarily, I am simply discharging the trust committed to me.*" In other words, if I do good with a sincere attitude I am going to be rewarded in heaven; but if I do the exact same thing without a good attitude, there will be no reward awaiting me when I get to heaven.

You see, God is not just concerned with what you do. He is genuinely concerned about your attitude when you do it. That is why it is so important to God that we are cheerful givers (see 2 Corinthians 9:7) rather than stingy, grumpy, grumbling givers. When we give, we can either do so grateful for the opportunity to sow into God's kingdom, or grumbling to ourselves about how we hate this part of service when the pastor talks about money! According to Paul, our attitude determines our reward.

1 John 1:7 says, *"But if we walk in the light as He is in the light, we have fellowship one with another."* Have you ever noticed that when you are living passionately for God and you get around someone else who is living passionately for God your spirits just kind of click? You are both moving in the same direction and serving the same God. The Bible calls that unity, and there is much power in unity.

In Matthew 18:19, Jesus said this about prayer: *"Again I say to you that if two of you agree on earth concerning anything that they ask, it will be done for them by My Father in heaven."* Jesus is saying that unity on earth reaches heaven.

The entire 133rd Psalm is about unity. Let's take a moment to read verses 1-3:

> *"Behold, how good and how pleasant it is for the brethren to dwell together in unity! It is like the precious oil upon the head, running down on the beard, the beard of Aaron, running down on the edge of his garments. It is like the dew of Hermon, descending upon the mountains of Zion; for there the Lord commanded the blessing—life forevermore."*

Did you notice that God commands blessing where there is unity? It is true in a church, it is true in your home, and it is true in your business.

I believe we often miss out on significant blessings because we don't have unity. I have talked to the staff of my church about this many times. They know that one of the quickest ways to find yourself looking for a new job is to be a promoter of strife and division. Proverbs 6:16 says there are six things the Lord hates, and the last one mentioned is spreading strife or division.

Did you notice the word picture about unity in Psalm 133? Verse 2 says, *"It is like the precious oil on the head running down on the beard.*" Unity starts at the head. Let's think about another simple, yet powerful, example: the family. Parents do not need to get into unity with their children. It is the children who are to get into unity with their parents. If you are a parent, you are responsible to set the course and bring them into agreement because unity starts at the head and moves down.

The story of Abraham in Genesis chapter 13 gives us a very powerful example of the blessing that comes from living in unity, as well as how to live in pursuit of unity. There we see how Abraham was blessed because of his covenant with God. We also learn that Lot, his nephew, was blessed because of his association with Abraham. In the same way Potiphar was blessed because Joseph was in his home,(Gen 39:5) so Lot was blessed because he was in Abraham's home. It is important to realize that the people with whom you choose to associate can cause you to miss or receive God's blessing.

Genesis 13:8-9 says, "*So Abram said to Lot, 'Please let there be no strife between you and me, and between my herdsmen and your herdsmen; for we are brethren. Is not the whole land before you? Please separate from me. If you take the left, then I will go to the right; or, if you go to the right, then I will go to the left.'*" Abram, the true cause of Lot's blessing, sees the strife that is building

THE MORE SPIRITUAL YOU ARE, THE QUICKER YOU'LL MOVE AWAY FROM STRIFE.

between their herdsmen and servants, so he goes straight to Lot to resolve the strife. The more spiritual you are, the quicker you'll move away from strife. The more spiritual person is also the one who is willing to pay the highest price to see unity achieved. Abraham let Lot take his pick of the land, and Lot picked the greenest land for himself. In the end, however, Abraham continues to be blessed, and it is Lot who loses everything.

Romans 12:18 says, "*If it is possible, as much as depends on you, live peaceably with all men.*" Unfortunately, some people will not have peace no matter what you do. It doesn't matter how kind you are to them, they will still be unhappy. However, as much as you possibly can, be the peacemaker.

Ephesians 4:3 talks about bearing with one another in love and, *"endeavoring to keep the unity of the Spirit in the bond of peace."* Did you notice the word endeavor? To endeavor is not something that is accomplished while lounging in your favorite recliner! When you endeavor to do something, it takes significant effort on your part; you are going to have to work at it.

James 3:16 (Amplified) says, *"For wherever there is jealousy (envy) and contention (rivalry and selfish ambition), there will also be confusion (unrest, disharmony, rebellion) and all sorts of evil and vile practices."* Keep in mind that it is the enemy who wants to bring disharmony to your home, relationships, and even your business.

Listen to Romans 16:17-18: *"I urge you, brethren, note those who cause divisions and offenses, contrary to the doctrine which you learned, and avoid them. For those who are such do not serve our Lord Jesus Christ, but their own belly, and by smooth words and flattering speech deceive the hearts of the simple."* Now notice verse 20: *"And the God of peace will crush Satan under your feet shortly."* Don't forget that it is Satan, not a person, with whom our struggle lies. Satan knows how damaging strife can be, and he will exploit it anytime you let him.

I strongly encourage you to take a lesson from Solomon. Seek genuine, sincere unity with those around you, confront strife and division. Don't let them in any area of your life.

CHAPTER 9

WISDOM AND TRUTH

"Do not speak in the hearing of a fool, for he will despise the wisdom of your words."

Proverbs 23:9

The first truth that stands out to me here is this: you and I should go where we are celebrated, not simply tolerated. If you are just tolerated where you work, you know it, and you should consider looking for a place where you will be celebrated.

There is another, more basic, truth being discussed here as well. That is the value of wisdom. In Proverbs 4:7, Solomon plainly states, *"Wisdom is the principle thing; therefore get wisdom. And in all your getting, get understanding."*

I like to define wisdom as the ability to see beforehand the outcome of a given set of actions. That foresight allows the wise to choose the best path. In many cases, it helps them avoid the school of hard knocks. For example, a 10 year-old boy who plays in the street but is very watchful and leaves at the first sign of a vehicle could be considered smart. However, if that same boy, realizing that he is capable of keeping himself safe, chooses to stay out of the street entirely because he can foresee his 3 year-old brother is likely to copy him by playing in the street as well but without any regard to the presence of cars, then he is wise. He was able to foresee the results of his decision.

With all the wonderful benefits of wisdom, you would expect it to be very popular. The Bible tells us that anyone can have it, yet it also says that most people do not hunger for it. You see, in order to obtain wisdom, one must pursue it. Wisdom is not the same as education. Someone can have so many degrees that their name looks like alphabet soup, but that doesn't guarantee that they have wisdom. It may indicate that they have a lot of knowledge, but it doesn't tell us if they sought wisdom as well as information.

Many people enjoy learning only what they can use to support the decisions they have already made. If you ever try to correct one of these people, they will most likely get mad. In Proverbs 1:24, wisdom is speaking and says, *"Because I have called and you refused, I have stretched out my hand and no one regarded, because you disdained all my counsel, and would have none of my rebuke."* Also in Proverbs 9:8 Solomon says, *"Do not correct a scoffer, lest he hate you; Rebuke a wise man, and he will love you."*

Have you noticed that we live in a society that does not want to be rebuked? No one wants to hear "that is wrong" or "that is not true." Proverbs makes it perfectly clear that if you listen to wisdom, you will hear the words "that is wrong, stop it." And when you do, you will listen. The wise man appreciates correction; the fool despises it.

I like the saying, "If the Bible rubs you the wrong way, turn around." Once, when the Apostle Paul was teaching his disciples and referring to some of the stories of the Israelites' many mistakes, he said, *"All these things happened to them as examples, and they were written for our admonition"* (1 Corinthians 10:11). "Admonition" sounds like such a polite word. If you look it up, though, one of its meanings is to "slap your face." That verse could read "These things are there to slap some sense into you." Many of us could use a good slap every once in a while. You might be considering doing something immoral, so you read about Samson, and SLAP! It hits you that sure, you could choose to do that immoral thing, but you'll regret it because it is eventually going to cost you.

Wisdom and truth are inseparable friends. That is because wisdom is the ability to foresee the benefit of accepting and walking in truth. Notice 2 Thessalonians 2:10 (NIV), which says: *"In every sort of evil that deceives those who are perishing. They perish because they refused to love the truth and so be saved."* Why were those people perishing? It was because they "refused to love the truth." They would not acknowledge the truth and accept that they were wrong. In order to be set free, you have to accept that you are bound.

In 2 Timothy 2:25, Paul was teaching about truth and correction. He wrote, *"Those who oppose him he must gently instruct, in the hope that God will grant them repentance leading them to a knowledge of the truth"* (NIV). You see, unless we repent, unless there is a change of mind, we cannot come to know truth. In the next chapter of Timothy, Paul used an example of some who refused to change their minds and believe the truth. He wrote, *"Now as Jannes and Jambres resisted Moses, so do these also resist the truth"* (2 Timothy 3:8-9).

WISDOM IS THE ABILITY TO FORESEE THE BENEFIT OF ACCEPTING AND WALKING IN TRUTH

You probably know who Jannes and Jambres are even if you didn't recognize their names. Remember in the Old Testament, when Aaron threw down his rod and God turned it into a snake? Jannes and Jambres were the magicians who, at Pharaoh's request, also turned their rods into snakes. Through demonic power they were able to produce supernatural results, but the truth of God's superiority was obvious when Aaron's snake ate both of theirs.

It is a beautiful picture of Jesus at Calvary. Let me explain: the two snakes that Aaron's snake gobbled up represented sin. Afterward, when Aaron grabbed the tail of his snake, it turned right back into a rod. It is just like when Jesus took your sin and then rose from the dead to return to God's right hand.

Jannes and Jambres, along with Pharaoh, had ignored the obvious truth even after going through plague after plague. They refused to repent because they were unwilling to accept the truth that stared them in the face. If you and I want to keep from making the mistakes others have made, we must stay open to God's correction in our lives and let Bible examples like this "slap" us in the face.

CHAPTER 10

SOWING AND REAPING, A JUDGE IN HEAVEN

*"Do not remove the ancient landmark, or enter the fields of
the fatherless; for their Redeemer is mighty; He will plead
their cause against you."*

Proverbs 23:10-11

You might remember that Solomon talked about ancient land-
marks a little earlier in Proverbs 23. However, this is not a repeat
of his previous point. Actually, he uses a similar example but wants
us to notice something new. This time, he wants to point out that
whatever you do, God sees it; and not only does God see it, but He
also repays.

We realize that in an earthly court we have the right to stand
before a judge and jury, but that doesn't mean justice is always served.
Not so with God. Galatians 6:7 says, *"Do not be deceived, God is not
mocked; for whatever a man sows, that he will also reap."* Some people
receive their just reward for sin now; others will receive it later. One
thing, however, is certain. Everyone will receive their just reward
sooner or later.

We need to remember that sin is not the only thing that is
repaid. In Revelations 22:12, John records Jesus as saying *"I am coming*

quickly, and My reward is with Me, to give to every one according to his work." Christians can become so focused on the fact that our works aren't what will get us into heaven that we fail to remember that we are going to be rewarded based on our works. In 1 Corinthians 3:10-15 we are told that there will be some who enter heaven but do not receive any rewards all. When you consider how long eternity is, doesn't it make sense to store up treasures there?

God says that He is the one who repays or rewards. He said, *"Vengeance is Mine, and recompense; their foot shall slip in due time; for the day of their calamity is at hand, and the things to come hasten upon them."* The question, then, is not whether justice will be served, but rather when and by whom it will be served. God asks us to leave the repayment to him.

So then, what do you do if someone does you wrong? What should you do if you don't see justice right away? According to the Bible, you forgive. That is, you let go of your right to impose punishment or hold a grudge, and you let God take care of it. And believe me, God can get even better than you or I ever could. You may think that the person you forgive is the one who most benefits from your forgiveness,

UNFORGIVENESS AFFECTS YOU. IT DISTORTS YOU, AND IT DISTORTS YOUR JUDGMENT.

but actually it is you who most benefits. Unforgiveness affects you. It distorts you, and it distorts your judgment. A prime example of unforgiveness distorting judgment is Judas and the decision he made to betray Jesus.

While Jesus and his disciples were in Bethany, they were enjoying a meal at the home of Simon the Leper (see Mark 14:3-9). As Jesus sat at the table, the Bible says that a woman entered with an alabaster box of perfume worth 300 denarii. At that time, if you worked from 6am to 6pm for one day, you could expect to be paid one denarii. Basically, the perfume she brought was worth 300 working days, or 14 months of wages. If we were to put a price tag on that today, assuming minimum wage, it would be nearly 20,000 dollars!

The woman took this costly box of perfume and poured it ALL out as she anointed Jesus. Some, including Judas Iscariot, became indignant, saying, *"Why was this fragrant oil wasted? It might have been sold… and given to the poor"* (Mark 14:4-5). Then Jesus rebuked them saying, *"Let her alone. Why do you trouble her? She has done a good work for Me. For you have the poor with you always, and whenever you wish you may do them good; but Me you do not have always. She has done what she could. She has come beforehand to anoint My body for burial"* (Mark 14:6-9).

Apparently all of this offended Judas. Walking in offense and unforgiveness crippled his judgment, and shortly thereafter he betrayed Jesus for thirty pieces of silver (see Matthew 26:15). Betraying the Son of God is a very bad decision, don't you agree? Unfortunately, it wasn't the first nor the last bad decision conceived in the fog of unforgiveness. The examples are endless, beginning with Cain and Abel and the first murder ever committed. Even today, wherever unforgiveness is given shelter, bad choices flock like pigeons to bread crumbs. I hope you can see how vital it is, if you have anything against anyone, let it go. Choose to forgive them, and let God handle the rest.

We have discussed leaving vengeance to God, but what about the reward that you know you deserve? Ephesians 6:7-8 (NIV) says, *"Serve wholeheartedly, as if you were serving the Lord, not men, because you know that the Lord will reward everyone for whatever good he does."* Ultimately, you should do everything you do for God. This can be easy to forget when you go to work and try to earn the bonus or win the promotion, but God is the one who will repay.

Have you ever poured yourself into something for your spouse, for your children, for a client, or for your boss only to have them shrug it off as if it was insignificant? When that happens, you have a choice to make. You can be hurt and offended because you are not appreciated and it seems like your effort isn't gaining you anything, or you can see the world as it truly is and realize that if you dedicate your effort to God, He will reward you. God never loses track of your hours or under-appreciates your effort. My favorite paraphrase of Ephesians 6:8 says, *"Whatever you make happen for others, God will make happen for you."* What a stress-free life we can live if we stop trying to keep score and extract repayment from everyone we have helped.

When I think of the importance of letting God handle our rewards, I can't help thinking about Joseph. Joseph started out as a diligent worker in his family's business, but instead of receiving acknowledgment and repayment, he was sold into slavery and his father was told he was dead. Joseph worked for Potiphar and brought God's blessing to his entire household. Just when it appeared that he was moving back up in the world, Potiphar's wife falsely accused him of attempted rape. Joseph was thrown into jail. That isn't exactly what I'd call a desirable compensation plan.

While in prison, Joseph worked diligently for the jailer who repaid his diligence with increased responsibility—but he was still in jail. One day, Pharaoh called on Joseph to interpret a dream. The Bible says that God gave Joseph wisdom and favor, and as a result he entered the throne room a prisoner and left as the prime minister of the most powerful country in the world! God doesn't always pay on Friday, but He does always pay!

CHAPTER 11

GROWING IN KNOWLEDGE

"Apply your heart to instruction, and your ears to words of knowledge."

Proverbs 23:12

The simplest definition of wisdom in Hebrew is "skill in living." Billy Graham said this: "Knowledge is horizontal, wisdom is vertical." What he means is that you can get knowledge from people, from a book, or from schooling. Wisdom, however, does not come from around you. It comes from above, from God, and we need wisdom to guide and guard us. So often we want an event, a special seminar, or even a single prayer to instantly make us wise. Wisdom, however, is not an event. It is a process, and wisdom comes daily from God to those who seek it.

You can think of it this way: wisdom does not go where it is needed; it goes where it is being sought. Jesus reiterates this truth for us, saying, *"Be careful what you are hearing. The measure [of thought and study] you give [to the truth you hear] will be the measure [of virtue and knowledge] that comes back to you—and more [besides] will be given to you who hear"* (Mark 4:24, AMP). What He is saying is that you need to spend time seeking God. You need to spend time in His Word because the more you attention you give to the revelation of God's truth the more revelation you will receive.

This is an important concept that many Christians either don't understand or simply ignore. A fantastic example of this is in Acts 10 where we find the account of Cornelius, a Roman Centurion who has accepted Judaism. He is praying and fasting when an angel appears to him and says, "*Send men to Joppa and have them bring back Simon Peter because he will tell you words by which you and all your household will be saved.*"(Acts 11:13) It is interesting that, when Cornelius did everything he knew to do, God made sure he learned more.

Author Joel Rosenberg tells of not just hundreds but hundreds of thousands of people throughout the Middle East coming to Jesus. The reports tell of how these people are actually having visions of Jesus coming to them and saying "I NISSA" which means "I am Jesus; the Messiah, I am the Savior." And these hungry "Muslims" are getting saved by the droves. How can this be? I believe these people sincerely walked in what light they had and God made sure they received more.

Far too often I hear people say, "I just don't think God is telling me anything, He seems so far away." I always ask them, "What is the last thing the Lord told you?" They usually tell me "I felt God said to do such and such." When I ask them, "Are you doing such and such?" they answer, predictably, "Well no, not really." It is not reasonable to think that God is going to keep revealing more and more truth and wisdom to you if you haven't done anything with the instruction

WHEN YOU WALK IN WHAT YOU CURRENTLY KNOW, YOU WILL NOT LACK FOR GOD'S DIRECTION FOR YOUR NEXT STEPS.

He previously gave you. When you walk in what you currently know, you will not lack for God's direction for your next steps.

The wisdom God has for you is not some "divine trivia" you can easily do without. Job 28:15-19 expounds on the value of wisdom telling us, "*It cannot be purchased for gold, nor can silver be weighed for its price. It cannot be valued in the gold of Ophir, in precious onyx or sapphire. Neither gold nor crystal can equal it, nor can it be exchanged for jewelry of fine gold. No mention shall be made of coral or quartz, for the price of wisdom is above rubies. The topaz of Ethiopia cannot equal it, nor can it be valued in pure gold"* (Job 28:15-19). This tells us that wisdom is more valuable than anything else on the planet!

Remember, we learned earlier that wisdom is the principal thing; therefore, we should get wisdom. Similarly, Proverbs 25:2 tells us that *"it is the glory of kings to search out a matter."* It should be our glory to seek after wisdom, too. God has hidden wisdom for you to find. He didn't hide wisdom so that it would remain undiscovered. Really, you could think of God as a parent who plays hide and seek with a preschool child. The parent hides just barely out of sight so that, as long as the child puts forth even a little effort, he is sure to find them. That is what God does with wisdom. God says if you seek wisdom, I will ensure that you will find it. However, I need to see some effort from you. You need to seek wisdom.

Here are four ways that we can "seek wisdom":

1. Pray for it. James 1:5 says, *"If any of you lacks wisdom, let him ask of God, Who gives to all liberally and without reproach, and it will be given to him."* Remember, God appeared to Solomon and asked him what he wanted, and Solomon said. "I want wisdom." Boy, did he get it! We also have God's promise that, if we ask for wisdom, He will deliver it to us.

2. Meditate on the Word of God. We just looked at Mark 4:24 *"The measure [of thought and study] you give [to the truth you hear] will be the measure [of virtue and knowledge] that comes back to you—and more [besides] will be given to you who hear"* (Mark 4:24, AMP). As you spend time meditating, knowledge and virtue will come to you. That is wisdom.

3. Walk in the light you already have. That may sound simple, but it is one of the biggest things stopping many Christians from growing any wiser or any stronger in their faith. Somewhere along the line they learned what God wants them to do, but they are unwilling to do it. Perhaps you have imagined that God wants you to do something big and extremely sacrificial like leaving everything you know to become a missionary in a third world country. Let me say this: usually it is something far less elaborate than that.

Like Naaman the leper, we are psychologically prepared to make big sacrifices, but when God asks something little of us, we feel justified in saying no (see 2 Kings, chapter 5). Most often, the thing that we failed to do is more like letting go of a grudge, or giving of your time or money. None-the-less, the reality is that as soon as we choose to withhold our obedience, no matter what the issue, we shut off the flow of wisdom and further revelation.

4. Through our associations. Proverbs 13:20 says, "*He who walks with wise men will be wise, but the companion of fools will be destroyed.*" The people we choose as our friends and constant companions will significantly affect our growth. Do the people you have surrounded yourself with spur you on to seek God and His truth? Or do your friends encourage you to feel comfortable with spiritual stagnation? Right voices in your life lead to right choices.

> **RIGHT VOICES IN YOUR LIFE LEAD TO RIGHT CHOICES.**

Most of us know people who, year after year, never seem to grow. They have kept the same dreams, but they never got past the same problems and the same excuses, the same alibis. They continue to ignore the same opportunities. They behave as if someday, through little or no effort of their own, they will win life's lottery and all their dreams will come true.

Nearly everyone desires success, but the difference is found in the willingness to pursue it, to seek wisdom. The apostle Paul wrote in Philippians 3:13, *"not that I count myself to have apprehended."* In other words, "I know that I have not arrived, but I am still seeking, still learning, still growing."

A wonderful example of willingness to pay the price of seeking knowledge can be found in the life of Dwight L. Moody. Perhaps you recognize his name. In the nineteenth century, Dwight L. Moody was one of the greatest evangelists in America. To this day, many schools and ministries still bear his name. However, during the height of his ministry, while in the middle of enormously successful campaigns in Great Britain and the United States, he realized he had become spiritually and intellectually malnourished. John Pollackwrites, "At the moment of reaching the height of influence in the United States, he stood in a dangerous spiritual insolvency. Moody realized that he had told people everything that he knew and that he had nothing new to say."

In a move that proves why God had trusted him with so much influence in the first place, Moody moved to Northfield and refused to accept major speaking engagements until he felt he had studied enough to have fresh, new insights from God's Word. He set a rigid schedule including six hours of study every morning. Even when he resumed his rigorous travel and speaking schedule, he began the practice of carrying a small library with him. He was determined that, in spite of the time-consuming press and the responsibilities his ministry required, he could not afford to stop learning if he expected to remain an effective spiritual leader.

Solomon reminds us that knowledge should be a lifelong pursuit. It is something we must intentionally and continuously seek to do. Will Rogers summed it up well when he said, "Even if you are on the right track, you will get run over if you just sit there."

CHAPTER 12

RAISING CHILDREN

"Do not withhold discipline from a child; if you punish him with the rod, he will not die."
Proverbs 23:13-14 (NIV)

Jeanie and I have four children who are now grown, and I am so thankful to say that they all love God and are pursuing the dreams He put in their hearts. However, we both will readily admit that it is not a result of our "single-handed perfect performance" as parents. Raising children is a job meant to be done along with God their Creator, and His "Instruction Manual"—the Bible. What an honor—and a relief—to work with Him raising up our children.

I thank God for the blessings he has given us in our children and, now, our grandchildren. Whenever I write a book, my wife is a big part of the process, but that is especially true in this chapter. Because she will have so much to add on this topic, I am going to change the format slightly. We will write this chapter as a team. Because I think it will be helpful for you to distinguish from whose perspective the comments and insights are coming, we will mark each time the writer changes with our names. I have witnessed my wife's daily requests for God's wisdom on this topic during decades of parenting, and I hope you enjoy gleaning from her wisdom and experience.

Jeanie:

I recently read an excerpt from a report on juvenile delinquency and how to avoid it. It was published by the state of Minnesota, and I regret that I did not note the date. The report stated: "Every baby starts life as a little savage; he's completely selfish and self-centered. A baby wants what he wants when he wants it. Deny him and he seethes with rage and aggressiveness which would be murderous were he not so helpless. Wrapped up in our children is the potential to be murderers and they need to be trained. They don't have morals, or knowledge, nor developed skills. This means that all children—not just certain ones—are born delinquent. If permitted to continue in their self-centered world of infancy, given full reign to their impulsive actions to satisfy every want, every child could grow up a criminal, a thief, a murderer, and a rapist."

Even this secular source recognized what the book of Proverbs says, that a child left to his own would bring his mother and father shame. (Proverbs 29:15) We are born without the wisdom to know how to live life appropriately with kindness and thoughtfulness. We must be trained in those things.

Duane:

Children, as the beginning scripture for this chapter points out, need discipline. The truth is they even want it. To illustrate my point, let me tell you a story about our youngest son, Daniel. It took place many years ago when he was about 8-years old. Our home was situated on the side of a small hill. My Ford Taurus was parked in front of the garage, and I left in a different vehicle to go somewhere. While Jeanie was in the house and no one else was around, Daniel climbed into the car, took the vehicle out of park, and released the parking brake. Naturally, gravity took over and the car rolled backwards down the hill with him in it! It ran over a small tree and ended up in a field. He didn't actually harm anything besides that little tree, but he knew that what he had done was wrong, and he knew he couldn't undo what he had done. He came into the house saying "Mommy, spank me; spank me, please spank me!"

Jeanie:

I didn't even know what he'd done, so I had to ask him, "Why do you need to be spanked?" It took a while for him to calm down enough to explain, but it was clear that he wanted his wrong to be made right. He wanted it to be paid for. He knew he would feel better when he could make things right again. He wanted to atone for what he had done.

Duane:

Malachi 2:15 says, "*But did He* (that's God) *not make them one?* (he is referring to a husband and a wife in marriage) *having a remnant of the Spirit? And why one? He seeks godly offspring.*" Some translations simply say, "*The purpose of marriage is to produce godly offspring, or godly seed.*"

Maybe you thought marriage was all about recreational companionship or perhaps the financial economy, sort of like carpooling through life. Although there are multiple reasons for marriage, God says the biggest reason is to raise godly children.

I want to remind you that the devil will always attack your seed. First, and foremost, your seed is your child(ren). It is also your faith, and according to 2 Corinthians chapter 9, your seed is also your finances. Jesus illustrated how Satan likes to attack while everything is still in seed or seedling form in the parable of the sower (see Mark 4:2-20). He will attack your finances, your faith, and your child(ren). Romans 7:23 indicates that "*the law of sin abides in our members,*" or in other words, there is an inclination inside of us to do wrong. I am guessing you have probably already noticed that the "law of sin" is also in your child(ren). You could say that this means that training them is an uphill battle.

That is why the Bible says, "Don't withhold discipline." Your children need discipline and, without it, the battle is already lost.

Because of the fall, sin abides in our members. Scripture literally says that if you give them discipline, you can "save their soul from death." Literally, you can save them from hell. (Proverbs 23:14)

Rebellion wants to control your kids. As a parent, it is your job to drive rebellion out. Some parents seem to think that if they can calmly endure being rebelled against, then what is the harm of letting their kid's rebel against them? After all, aren't they only hurting the parent who is willing to endure it?

The problem is that rebellion, according to 1 Samuel 15:23, is, *"as the sin of witchcraft"*—it is a demonic presence. As such, rebellion is not just focused on the parent. A child will not be rebellious toward their parents, and then go out and be submissive toward God or other authority figures. Outwardly, it may appear that way for a time, but on a heart level, that isn't possible. Eventually, external actions will follow the heart. If there is rebellion, it will enter all realms of authority. There are three realms of authority: divine, governmental, and family. Rebellion in any of these areas will quickly overflow to the others. That is why Solomon said that discipline will save their souls from death or hell. If we allow rebellion in our home, it will turn to rebellion in our children's hearts toward God.

A CHILD WILL NOT BE REBELLIOUS TOWARD THEIR PARENTS, AND THEN GO OUT AND BE SUBMISSIVE TOWARD GOD OR OTHER AUTHORITY FIGURES.

Jeanie:

Throughout Proverbs, Solomon refers to the "simple" and the "fool." The simple is someone who is without moral direction and inclined toward evil. Until we learn God's Word from our parents or somewhere—that describes all of us. It is human nature. There is no need to teach your children to be selfish. I remember when our daughter Stephanie was a baby. We put her in the nursery at church, and when I went to pick her up the nursery worker was holding Stephanie, who had a big grin on her face. However, the nursery worker was not smiling; she was scowling. On the other side of the room, with another of the workers, was a little boy in tears. As she handed me my baby, she said, "Your daughter just bit that little boy." It turns out that the little boy had a toy that Stephanie wanted, so she bit him and took it from him. I never taught her to do that. She came up with that idea entirely on her own. Like all of us, she was born with an inclination toward sin. She needed training.

A fool is one who has gone beyond an inclination to evil and has now chosen to embrace evil. Psalms 53:1 says, "*The fool has said in his heart, "There is no God."*" That is the last thing we would ever want to hear our children say. In Proverbs 22:15, Solomon tells us, "*Foolishness is bound up in the heart of a child; the rod of correction will drive it far from him.*"

As parents, we are clearly warned against withholding discipline. We are not supposed to keep from our children the benefit of being corrected, of being warned, of being instructed, of being restrained, and of being chastened. This is something that every child needs in order to grow and mature to become a healthy productive adult.

We need to be careful about what we allow to shape our practices as parents. It is very easy to allow the impressions that we get from society to direct us. In this internet age, it easy to find articles, websites, and people who will agree with just about any parenting approach you could dream up. There are many parenting philosophies, complete with books written by credentialed psychologists, which will tell you the exact opposite of what the Bible does. They will say that children are basically good, and that, left on their own they will become the greatest versions of themselves. They will argue that discipline damages the child, but the Bible says that just isn't true.

As a Christian parent, you must decide if you will trust God who made your child and knows him or her inside and out or popular culture, which changes every few months. Will you trust your children to the advice of "experts" who insist their method works just because it fits their newly invented view of life? Why would you want to trust someone who, whenever their method doesn't work, simply says "they are going through a phase"?

It is never okay to abuse a child. We have been entrusted with a precious and vulnerable gift in our children. God is clear, however, that to lovingly discipline your child in the hopes of saving them from the rebellion that will otherwise takeover is not abuse. It will not harm them.

DO NOT CORRECT YOUR CHILDREN IN ANGER

You must be careful, however, and I encourage you, do not correct your children in anger.

Consider this: there is a type of abuse that our culture will not even admit exists. It is abuse nonetheless. What is this unnamed abuse? It is when parents leave their child without direction or correction. It is when parents leave children to themselves to follow the dictates of their rebellious nature within. The Bible is clear that the "simple" need to be guided, corrected, and trained to become wise.

Our government understands that, before you let a teenager loose with a car, they need to have rules and instructions. Your children aren't allowed to jump into any old vehicle and drive it anywhere they feel like. They need to be trained and equipped. They need to learn that their actions will have consequences. Society agrees that training, correction, and consequences are necessary for a teenager to become equipped to drive a car. In the same way, our children need to be equipped, trained, and corrected to be able to handle life, to stay on the road of life, and to stay on the moral path. When we correct our children we *"deliver their souls from death."* (Proverbs 23:14)

Duane:

It is clear in scripture that God has given to the parents a responsibility to teach their children. In 1 Samuel 3:13 it is talking about Eli the high priest who raised the prophet Samuel. Eli had children of his own who became extremely ungodly. The verse says *"For I have told him that I will judge his house forever for the iniquity which he knows, because his sons made themselves vile, and he did not restrain them."* A parent is not responsible for every individual choice that his grown children make, but in this case God recognized that Eli had so neglected his parental responsibility to restrain his children that Eli was held responsible and his whole house was judged for the wicked actions of his children. Eli was partly to blame because he had failed to parent as he should.

As Jeanie mentioned, we are instructed to use the rod of correction. Proverbs 22:15 *"Foolishness is bound up in the heart of a child; but the rod of correction will drive it far from him."* It must be administered in love—because we love them—to correct and direct away from wrong choices. Although the scriptures say to use a rod, it is for correcting, NOT because we're just "fed up," inconvenienced or angry at them. And it is not the only way that we have to train our children. But if we choose to follow political correctness instead of scripture and exclude it entirely, we are clearly ignoring scripture.

We must also love our children. Proverbs 13:24 says *"He who spares his rod hates his son, But he who loves him disciplines him promptly."* Our discipline of our kids is to always be based in love not anger.

Of course it is natural to feel angry when you find the only picture of your deceased grandfather was being used as a dart board. (Yes, that happened at our home). But, as parents, we must learn to deal with our tempers before dealing with our kids. Punishment should have nothing to do with anger. Instead it is to protect them from the consequences of rebellion and

WE MUST LEARN TO DEAL WITH OUR TEMPERS BEFORE DEALING WITH OUR KIDS

wrongdoing. It is because we love our children that we correct them. Sometimes you just have to wait—as long as it takes—to cool off. Then come back and instruct, teach, and discipline the child who needs a reminder of how to live right. They need to be instructed, but we need reminded as parents that if we discipline in anger we are crippling our own efforts. The most effective discipline is biblical discipline, and that means it is done in love.

The "rod of correction" follows a broken rule—not a childish behavior, mistake, or mishap. Parents, first make sure that the kids understand what is expected and know what the consequences will be if they disobey. If they choose to disobey, you can then respond without anger and remind them of the reason for the "consequences" and that you are on their side, wanting to help them make the better choice next time. Let them hear the scripture that tells them to obey (Ephesians 6:1, 2) "*Children obey your parents in the Lord, for this is right… that it may go well with you and that you may enjoy long life…*" Then in love administer the rod of correction. Afterwards you reinforce your love for them. You make it clear to them that you are not angry with them.

CHAPTER 13

JOY & THE POWER OF WORDS

"My son, if your heart is wise, my heart will rejoice indeed, I myself; Yes, my innermost being will rejoice when your lips speak right things"

Proverbs 23:15-16

Proverbs 18:21 expounds on this same principle when it says *"Death and life are in the power of the tongue and they that love it will eat the fruit thereof."*

It is important for us to realize that we are physical and spiritual beings living in a physical and spiritual world and that the words that we speak are more than noise. Our words can literally determine success or failure.

The right word at the right time is very powerful. Isaiah 50:4 *"the servant of God says 'The Lord God has given me the tongue of a disciple and one who is taught that I should know how to speak a word in season to him who is weary."* When someone is depressed and discouraged, the right words can lift them up.

Job was going through, literally, the trial of his life. His three friends show up and begin to attack him and make false accusations against him. Even in the middle of it all Job says, *"How forceful are right words."* (Job 6:25) There in the midst of trial Job acknowledges that the right words would make a huge difference.

In the New Testament the angel that appeared to Cornelius speaks of how powerful words are when he said "He (Peter) will tell you words by which you and your household will be saved." The very act of salvation involves hearing and accepting, as truth, the right words. The power to turn a bad situation around in your life often involves hearing and accepting the right words. Perhaps the most classic Biblical example is found in Numbers chapter 13. Here the children of Israel have come to the edge of the Promised Land to a place called Kadesh Barnea. Moses sends out 12 spies and tells them "Go and see what the land is like and bring back some of its fruit." The spies go and the land is even more wonderful than they expected. The Bible says that in the valley of Eshcol they cut a cluster of grapes so large it was carried on a pole between two men. (Today in Israel the image of two men carrying a cluster of grapes can be found on some of their coins.)

When the spies return from having fully scouted the land ten of the spies say "The land is as wonderful as God said it would be BUT the people who dwell in the land are strong and the cities are fortified and very large; moreover we saw the descendants of Anak there (Anak by the way and his descendants were giants) "we also saw the Amalekites, the Hittites, the Jebusites, the Amorites, and the Canaanites." The ten spies finish by saying "We are not able to go up against the people for they are stronger than we." Only two of the spies, namely Joshua and Caleb, say "Let us go up at once for we are well able to overcome it."

The ten spies respond by saying "There were giants there. We were like grasshoppers in our own sight and so we were in their sight." They had what I call the "grasshopper complex." They chose to see themselves the way they believed they were being seen by those around them. Only two spies were wise enough to recognize that it is God's perspective, not those of the inhabitants in the land, that mattered most.

Unfortunately the people believed the "evil report" of the ten spies instead of the faith filled accurate report of Joshua and Caleb. The Israelites began to complain. They said *"If only we had died in the land of Egypt! Or if only we had died in this wilderness! Why has the Lord brought us to this land to fall by the sword that our wives and children should become victims? Would it not be better for us to return to Egypt?"* (Numbers 14:2-3).

Then in chapter 28 verse 14 God Himself enters the conversation *"Just as you have spoken in My hearing so I will do to you."* Everyone received exactly what they said. Two million people said "We cannot go in, it would be better to die in the wilderness" and so they did. Two men said we are well able to enter, and of all who were above 20 years of age they were the only two who ever did. The Israelites remained in the desert for forty years while all those who complained died off.

It is interesting to note that when Joshua is finally leading the Israelites back into the Promised Land to take the city of Jericho he doesn't allow any opportunity for complaining. He instructs the people for the entire time they are following God's peculiar battle plan of marching around the city "Not to speak a word." Knowing that human nature was the same then as today, I believe that if he had allowed discussion during those marches the Israelites might have complained themselves out of the Promised Land a second time. It would have been very easy for everyone to begin to second guess Joshua's orders as they marched around the city, and saw how well fortified it was. Few battle plans have ever been easier to criticize than that one. I can all too easily imagine them saying "This is totally ridiculous and…." Good thing they weren't allowed to speak because if they had begun to speak those doubts, fears and negativity they would have been right back where their parents had been 40 years before. Instead Joshua said "Don't say anything until the horns of the high priest blow and then I want you to shout!"

The Israelites, it seems, did learn a lesson about the power of words and the danger of negativity and murmuring. History tells us it became standard procedure for the High Priest to stand in front of the soldiers before they left for battle and say "If you are afraid, go home: just go home because we don't want you telling others how afraid you are because that will put fear in their hearts."Of the virtuous woman in Proverbs 31 the Bible says *She opens her mouth with wisdom and on her tongue is the law of kindness.* We live in a culture today of toxic parents. It is sadly common for children to be told by their parents things like "You are so stupid you will never amount to anything." "Can't you do anything right?" "They must have messed up in hospital because I know my own kid would never do that!" These kids then spend their life trying to overcome the words that have been spoken over them. Instead they should be fulfilling the blessings their parents spoke over them.

Psalms 77 says *I complained and my spirit was overwhelmed.* It is a spiritual reality that if you say the wrong things it can literally cause you to be overwhelmed. Many people who feel overwhelmed honestly believe it is their situation that overwhelmed them. They think their speech is just a reflection of the situation. That argument only appears to be valid if the complainer never looks beyond themselves. First and foremost even a glance into God's Word tells us our words bring either death or life. But also when we look around we will realize that many people have encountered similar, if not worse, circumstances. Many people who have much more challenging circumstances are in fact more content than those who speak negatively about their less challenging situations. Those who chose to consistently speak God's blessing

IT IS A SPIRITUAL REALITY THAT IF YOU SAY THE WRONG THINGS IT CAN LITERALLY CAUSE YOU TO BE OVERWHELMED.

instead of complaining are not overwhelmed or depressed like their complaining counterparts. Psalms describes it this way *"Yea though I walk through the valley of death I will fear no evil for You are with me."*

As a former missionary I have accompanied many people the first time they see extreme poverty. We visited churches in towns with no electricity and stayed with pastors whose homes have dirt floors… Countless times I have witnessed Americans as they are faced with the radical reality that contentment doesn't come from your surroundings, it comes from God and is a result of your words and thoughts.

I would like to close this chapter with a quote from Max Lucado, "You have the ability with your words to make a person stronger; your words are to their soul what vitamins are to their body. And if you had food and saw someone starving wouldn't you share it? If you had water and saw someone dying of thirst wouldn't you give it? Of course you would. Then won't you do the same for their heart? Your words are food and water. Don't withhold encouragement from the discouraged; do not keep affirmation from the beaten-down. Speak words that make people stronger; believe in them as God has believed in you."

CHAPTER 14

BE ETERNALLY MINDED

*"Don't let your heart envy sinners but always be zealous
for the fear of the Lord. For there is surely a future hope for
you, and your hope will not be cut off."*
Proverbs 23:17-18

The command sounds easier said than done "Do not let your heart envy sinners." Some people will read this and think "But how can I obey that? How can I control what I feel?" Controlling your emotions is a foreign concept to many people in today's society. Jesus said it can be done. In fact, He told us to do it when he said *"Don't let your heart be troubled"* (John 14:1). It can be difficult when our society, and especially Hollywood, constantly feeds us stories that celebrate the person who follows their emotions instead of their commitments or the rules. Over and over the story is shown us of a protagonist who follows their feelings, or as Hollywood often calls it their heart, and it eventually leads them to happily ever after. Our society promotes the idea that to find out who you really are, just listen to your emotions. The ridiculousness of the world's approach is obvious when society tells a man "if you feel like a woman you must be one." That is insane. If I am a man it doesn't matter if I feel like woman, or a squirrel, I am still a man. God, in stark contrast with today's culture says "If you want to know who I made you to be, ask

Me. I have put in detail who you are and what you need to be fulfilled right there in the Bible."

When culture and the Bible disagree you need to decide right now, if you haven't already who you are going to believe. Your emotions are not an uncontrollable force to which you are enslaved. The main thing that shapes your emotions are your thoughts. I believe on some level we all realize that. Our emotions will always move in the direction of our dominant thought. If we just allow any thought at any time to enter our mind our emotions will follow those thoughts. It will feel very much

YOUR EMOTIONS ARE NOT AN UNCONTROLLABLE FORCE TO WHICH YOU ARE ENSLAVED.

like our emotions were random and out of control. But the Bible tells us we are to be careful about what we think on. Philippians 4:8 says *"What so ever things are pure, what so ever things are just, what so ever things are of a good report, think on these things."*

Elijah the Tishbite was a prophet of God. First, he prophesies that there will be no rain until he says so, and immediately there is a drought. During that time God feeds him miraculously by a raven that brings him bread and meat everyday twice a day. Then, God sends him to a widow's home where in a continuous miracle God causes their tiny supply of oil and flour to always replenish. After that, he goes to Mount Carmel where in the presence of witnesses he calls fire down from heaven that consumes the offering. He kills 450 prophets of Baal. He climbs to a mountain top and prays that rain would come and end the three and a half year drought. As the rain approaches, he tells the king to race 18 miles home in his horse drawn chariot. God's spirit comes on Elijah and he out runs the king's horses over those same 18 miles! Elijah is definitely on a roll. However when Jezebel hears what Elijah did to her prophets of Baal she sends a message to him saying "The gods do so to me and more if you are not dead like one of those prophets by this time tomorrow."

After such an impressive string of supernatural events you would probably expect Elijah to shrug off her threat, but instead scriptures says "When he saw that he was stricken with fear." He ran three days in the desert, sat under a tree and begged that God would kill him. Notice that when he heard the description of Jezebel's threat it says "He saw that." Have you ever noticed that we think in pictures? If you hear the words "three-headed dog" your mind creates an image of a three-headed dog. Elijah's mind created an image of the fulfillment of Jezebel's threat and he chose to keep that image in the forefront of his mind. His emotional reactions of fear and panic, even his suicidal desires, all came from his choice to continuously think about and envision Jezebel's threat coming to reality. He had plenty of positive things he could have focused on but, like many others who struggle with depression he didn't do it.

In the 73rd Psalm David speaks a bit about envying sinners in verse 11. He says *"And they say 'How does God know? Is there knowledge in the Most High' behold, these are the ungodly who are always at ease, they increase in riches."* In verse 17 David gives us the key to solving that apparent dilemma of the over privileged sinner. *"Until I went in to the Sanctuary of God; then I understood their end. Surely You set them in slippery places; You cast them down to destruction. Oh, how they are brought to desolation as in a moment they are utterly consumed with terror."* David is reminding us that it is all about perspective. When Job looked at the destiny of the unjust from God's perspective, which includes the present but also includes eternity, suddenly he was reminded that the success he thought he saw was only a temporary drop in the bucket. We must keep an eternal perspective. When looked at in its entirety there is no longer any reason to be envious of the plight of the unjust.

In this saying Solomon continues: "Always be zealous for the fear of the Lord." A prerequisite to being capable of obeying this command is to always be in the Word of God. Jesus was very clear in Matthew 4:4 *"Man shall not live by bread alone but by every word that proceeds out of the mouth of God."* Psalm 1:2 also says "But his delight is in the law of the Lord and in His law he meditates day and night."

Secondly, to maintain zeal for God we must do the work of the Lord. Romans 12:11 says *"Don't let your enthusiasm wane—be spiritually alive,—binding yourself to the Lord in service."* If the only thing you ever do is attend church it is good that you go but that is not enough for you to develop properly. Christianity is not just a meal ticket into eternity. Jesus repeatedly refers to the kingdom of heaven as being here and now. I am not claiming the millennial reign has begun. I realize that the millennial reign will be the most complete display of God's kingdom here on earth. But, scripture does not say that God's kingdom starts in the millennium. Scripture says that it is already here and that we are to participate with our gifts and talents as a part of the body of Christ.

Revelation 22:12 clearly shows us that when Jesus returns he expects that we will have been working. *"Behold I'm coming quickly; My reward is with me to give to everyone according to his work."*

As Solomon finishes verse 18 he says *"For surely there is a hereafter and your hope will not be cut off."* There is a future hope for you. There is a heaven to gain and a hell to shun. He is reminding us of the certainty of eternity and the spirit realm. The temptation is to think of the spirit realm as something mystical and somehow less real than the physical. The truth is that the spirit world created the natural world. It was here before the natural world and it will be here afterwards. What makes humans so special is that we are a hybrid being. Angels are purely spiritual and animals are purely natural. You, however, have a part of you that is most at home in the spiritual realm and a part that is most at home in the natural realm.

Heaven will be a wonderful place. There is no bad part of heaven. However everyone there is not fully satisfied. Paul tells us in Corintians 5:2 that *"you will long to be clothed."* You see, if you die before Jesus returns and resurrects the dead the part of you that is natural is still dead. Paul says that you will long to be "clothed" or reunited with that body. It is interesting to note that it is because of this that Christians have always buried their dead instead of cremating them, as many pagan societies do. When Moses died God buried him, he didn't cremate him. I am not saying God cannot resurrect the body of the cremated. Of course he can. I don't know how He does it. I suppose it will be like the many Christian martyrs that were burned at the stake. My point, however, is that Christians should be spiritually minded even in their natural choices. The percentage of Americans who choose cremation has increased from 1.5% in 1900 to 3% in 1960 and then jumped to near 33% today. This is representative of the disassociation with the spirit realm that plagues Christianity today. Christians in America have lost sight of the spiritual significance of many of their choices including burial, which ideally should be a symbol of their faith in the coming resurrection.

1 Thessalonians 5:23 says *"Now may the God of peace Himself sanctify you completely and may your whole spirit, soul, and body be preserved blameless at the coming of our Lord Jesus Christ."* God is obviously interested in both your spiritual and natural body. In Acts 7:60 it is talking about Stephen and it says *"And they stoned him and he fell asleep."* It is almost a certainty that because he was stoned his skull was crushed, so why would scripture say of his body that "he fell asleep"? The reason the Bible says it that way is because just like your body goes to sleep each night only to wake up the next morning, so our bodies in death go to sleep to eventually be awakened or resurrected by God Himself.

One reason I believe many Christians are not eternally minded is because they just don't know enough about what eternity will be like. I have heard Christians say things like "I am glad to be saved and all but I am not looking forward to floating around heaven on a cloud." Most of us remember that in heaven there is no suffering, no sin, and none of the consequences of the fall. But what about the things that are there? The Bible tells us that Heaven will be a place of reunion and fellowship. There will be music, trees, lakes, rivers, and homes. "That sounds like earth" you may say. That is right, heaven will be a lot like earth but without the effects of sin. In fact,

Revelation shows us that those who died before Jesus' return will be coming back to a new and improved earth for the 1000 year millennium. There is a lot to look forward to in eternity, and a lot we can do now to prepare for it.

PREPARING YOUR HEART

"My child listen and be wise; keep your heart on the right course"

Proverbs 23:19a

Notice that God places the responsibility for the course of our hearts on us. We often want to saddle God with the responsibility for making our choices for us with prayers that say "Lord make me this or make me that." If you ask to be a person of prayer and the Word, God won't force you out of bed each morning to spend the necessary time reading and praying. You will need to set your alarm, choose not to hit snooze, and be diligent about it. If you pray a prayer like "God make me an honest person" you will still be responsible to choose to tell the truth. The Holy Spirit can remind you in the moment of your commitment to be honest but the responsibility for your choice and for the preparation of your heart is yours.

2 Chronicles 12:14 says *"And he did evil because he did not prepare his heart to seek the Lord:"* The clear implication is that if he had prepared his heart then he would have done what was right. In this chapter I am going to give eight steps to preparing your heart. Your heart is really a combination of your soul and your spirit. Jeremiah 17:9 says, *"The heart is deceitful above all things and desperately wicked; who can know it?"*

Another scripture that will serve as foundation before we enter our list of steps is James 1:27, *"Pure and undefiled religion before God the Father is this: to visit orphans and widows in their trouble, and to keep oneself unspotted from the world."* How is it that you will be "unspotted"? The Bible says "You will keep yourself," As we already noticed, it is not God who does it for you. Someone wise once described it this way "It starts with a thought. If you don't guard that thought, it will produce an action. That action will produce a habit, and your habits will produce your destiny." As you can see it all starts with your thoughts, and what you allow your heart to meditate on.

Here are eight steps to "keeping" or as I like to call it "preparing your heart."

1. Take time every day to pray.

I have told my church for years that your heart turns towards the one that you pray to as well as those you pray for. As you pray to God your heart turns toward God. There is a strength that you receive when you pray. Prayer is simply talking to God. It doesn't always have to be something fancy. Sometimes a simple "God I need your help" is what we need. But I want to encourage you to take advantage of some of the amazing prayers that the Bible shows us. There is no better prayer book than the Bible itself.

The prayers in the Bible are God-breathed and we can be 100% sure we are praying God's will when we pray these prayers. One of these prayers can be found in Ephesians 3:14, I would encourage you to pray this prayer for yourself daily. Paul describes here how he prays for the Ephesians. *"For this reason I bow my knee to the Father of our Lord Jesus Christ from whom the whole family of heaven and earth is named. That He would grant you according to the riches of His glory to be strengthened with might through His Spirit in the inner man. That Christ may dwell in your hearts through faith that you, being rooted and grounded in love, may be able to comprehend with all the saints what is width, the length, the depth, the height; to know the love of Christ that passes knowledge; that you may be filled with all the fullness of God."*

That prayer is a lot different than just "Lord bless me." It has real spiritual substance. The great thing is that it is an inspired prayer that God will answer in your life.

There are prayers that I pray for my family; there are prayers I pray for my church, 365 days a year. It is not something God will make you do. You prepare your heart.

Another power-packed Biblical prayer is found in Colossians 1:9. It says *"For this reason we also since the day we heard of it did not cease to pray for you and to ask that you may be filled with the knowledge of His will in all wisdom and spiritual understanding. That you may walk worthy of the Lord, fully pleasing Him, being fruitful in every good work and increasing in the knowledge of God. Strengthened with all might according to His glorious power for all patience and long suffering with joy."* Wow! There is so much substance to those biblical prayers. Remember, God isn't going to make you a person of prayer; you must make one of yourself. You must become disciplined.

2. Be a doer of the Word.

James 1:22 *"But be doers of the Word and not hearers only deceiving your selves; for if anyone is a hearer of the Word and not a doer, he is like a man observing his natural face in a mirror; for he observes himself, goes away, and immediately forgets what kind of man he was. But he who looks into the perfect law of liberty and continues in it, and is not a forgetful hearer but a doer of the Word, this one will be blessed in what he does."* Many Christians act as if by sitting through a sermon and hearing something, that what they heard is now a part of their life. The Bible is very clear. If you hear or know something but do not act on it then you "deceive yourself." It isn't a part of your life when you hear it, it becomes are part of your life only when you do it.

The Bible says if you hear but you don't do, you are like a person who gets up in the morning, looks in the mirror to see that their hair is a mess, their eyes are red and puffy, and there is a crusty on their nose. After seeing all that they turn around and go to work as if everything was in order. Seeing the problem did them no good at all if they weren't willing to do anything about it. God's Word is like a mirror in which we view our life. When we put our life in front of God's Word the areas we need to make adjustments will stand out. It is not the act of learning that benefits us; it is our reaction to what we learn. To hear and not do is to be self-deceived.

> # IT IS NOT THE ACT OF LEARNING THAT BENEFITS US; IT IS OUR REACTION TO WHAT WE LEARN.

Hosea 10:12 says *"Sow for yourselves righteousness, reap in mercy; break up your fallow ground for it»s time to seek the Lord until He come and rain righteousness on you."* To understand the scripture we need to understand the term "fallow ground." Since not many of us are farmers I will explain. Fallow ground is ground that was once used but then was left alone and has gone back to packed earth and weeds. In order to use it for production again you literally have to break it up, re-prepare it. That happens often in our lives as well. There are areas we have allowed weeds to grow up, good habits that we have perhaps abandoned. You need to *"break up your fallow ground; it is time to seek the Lord until He comes and rains righteousness on you."*

The third verse of Jude also talks about the effort following God's Word will require of us. *"Beloved, while I was very diligent to write to you concerning our common salvation, I found it necessary to write to you, exhorting you to contend earnestly for the faith which was once for all delivered to the saints."* In other words, Paul is saying that you will have to fight or "contend earnestly" to maintain the truth of the message of your salvation. I believe God was warning us that over the centuries somehow there would be times when parts of the Church would back away from the truth that is found in the Bible. They would say things like "this part has passed away and is no longer applicable today." The church as a whole, however, will have to fight for truth, sometimes re-plowing areas where weeds have grown up from lack of use.

Just as this is applicable to the Church as a whole, it also applies to each of us individually. The enemy will come just like he came to Eve and say "Has God really said.... You won't really die." Satan will say to you, "That thing you have been doing, it isn't really working, it isn't really what God demands of you. You can get away with doing much less." We need to actively choose to be doers of the Word that we receive and actively search for areas where we have let things slip and where we need to break up the fallow ground.

3. Confession is the third way we prepare our heart.

Proverbs 23:13 *"He who covers his sin will not prosper, but whoever confesses and forsakes them will have mercy."* When you just keep on going in the direction that you're going, ignoring what you know is right, your heart literally grows harder and harder towards God. What you need is to confess and forsake, not cover and excuse.

1 John 1:8 *"If we say we have no sin we deceive ourselves and the truth is not in us. If we confess our sins he is faithful and just to forgive us our sins and to cleanse us from all unrighteousness"*

The Bible is very clear that if there is something in our life that shouldn't be there, we need to confess that sin and forsake it. God says if we take that step, He will cleanse us of unrighteousness and best of all He ensures us we will find mercy.

Hosea chapter 14 says nearly the same thing *"Take words with you and return to the Lord. Say to Him 'take away all our iniquity; receive us graciously for we will offer the sacrifice of our lips'."*

When we hear the term "confession" most of us think of the confession of sins. That is not, however, the only type of biblical confession. There is the confession of Jesus Christ as Lord of your life, which is how you received salvation. There is the confession of the Word of God. Joshua 1:8 says *"This book of the law shall not depart out of your mouth."* Philemon 1:6 says *"That the sharing of your faith may become effective by the acknowledgment of every good this which is in you in Christ Jesus."* The King James Version calls it the communication of your faith.

Preparing our hearts goes beyond confessing our sins to the Lord. We should acknowledge verbally who we are in Christ Jesus. We should confess what scripture tells us, that we are the head and not the tail; we are above and not beneath; we are healed, and delivered. Beyond confession of sin we need to confess who we are in Christ; what belongs to us in Christ; and our position in Christ.

4. Keep the right company.

1 Corinthians 15:33 *"Don't be deceived; evil company corrupts good habits or good morals"* I have seen people use that scripture to justify being isolated. Sampson is a good example of someone who got in trouble by isolating himself. I preached a sermon once titled "Sampson, the Lone Ranger." He was such a loner that he had to hire 30 people to pose as his friends at his wedding. His lack of good relationships is a large part of why he got in so much trouble. He needed a friend to talk him out of some of his crazy ideas.

David's son Amnon is another classic example of the consequences of bad friendships. The Bible says that Amnon becomes infatuated with his half-sister Tamar. When he tells his friend about his obsession, instead of telling him to snap out of it, the friend gives him a wicked plan of how to realize his twisted fantasy. The friend advises him to pretend he is sick and to request of the king that his sister prepare him some food. When she brings it to him and they are alone he rapes her. YUCK! The trouble doesn't stop there. The stupid idea Amnon

RIGHT VOICES BRING RIGHT CHOICES

had, and the wicked encouragement his degenerate friend gave him, literally got him killed. Tamar's brother Absalom was so furious about what Amnon did that later he killed him. If he would have had a good friend who would say "What is wrong with you? She is your sister!" He would have lived much longer.

Remember, right voices bring right choices.

5. Be a part of a vibrant local church.

Hebrews 10:25 *"Not forsaking the assembling of ourselves together as is the manner of some, but exhorting one another and so much the more as you see the day approaching."* Notice that Jesus didn't say that Christians would gradually no longer need church. In fact He said the opposite, *"So much the more as you see the day approaching."* Jesus says that our need for Christian fellowship will grow stronger in the end, not weaker. He also said "I will build my church and the gates of hell will not prevail against it." Are you wondering what Jesus is doing? He is building the church. You can judge the condition of the kingdom of God in a community by the strength of the local church. The church, according to scripture, is the hope of the world.

Some people say, "I can be a better Christian from home, I don't need church." What they are really saying is "I know more than the Bible does about being a Christian." When Jesus appears in the Bible He speaks to the church; He speaks to the church at Ephesus, and then the church at Philadelphia. He is building the church and we need to be a part of what Jesus is doing in the earth. We don't attend church because it is perfect or because everyone there is flawless without any hypocrisy whatsoever. We attend because Jesus said to. Because the church is what He is building on earth. It is where he is putting his energy, and because scripture tells us it will benefit us greatly.

6. Make sure you take time to be a worshiper.

Jesus said in John chapter 4:24 *"God is Spirit and they that worship Him must worship Him in spirit and in truth."* Worship is more than just repeating certain pleasant words. It is your spirit connecting spirit to spirit with God. I have seen the spirit of God do more in a few seconds of worship than a psychiatrist can accomplish in hundreds of hours on their couch.

Music is more than just sounds; it is spiritual, and can either lead us toward God or away from Him. The first time in the Bible anyone was delivered of an evil spirit was during worship. King David who was not yet king was worshiping with his harp in the presence of King Saul and scripture says that the evil spirit departed out of him. On the other hand, Nebuchadnezzar erected a ninety foot tall image of gold in direct rebellion against a dream God had given him where his kingdom was only the head of gold. He then invites all of the leaders from his provinces to gather and says to them, *"When you hear the music"* and then lists about ten instruments, *"then you bow down and you worship the image that I have made."* King Nebuchadnezzar understood something most of us don't realize: music is spiritual. Music opens you up to the spirit realm, both the divine realm or the demonic realm. He knew that through music he could get people to do things that they would otherwise not do. Similarly when the Spirit of God is in worship, He will touch your heart and help you surrender to God, even to make commitments that you probably would not have made without the spiritual inspiration of the music.

7. Giving; Sow into the Kingdom of God.

Matthew 6:21 *"For where your treasure is, there your heart will be also."* Simply put if your treasure, which is your wealth, is not invested in the Kingdom of God then your heart won't be either. We are talking about ways that we can prepare our hearts, or as Solomon said "Keep our hearts on course." The choices you make concerning how and where you invest your hard earned money are one of the closest things to a steering wheel your heart may have. You can turn your heart by putting your treasure where you want your heart to go.

I remember when we bought a piece of land and began building our home on that property. Before purchasing that land I didn't know that street existed, but during the time when we were putting so much of our "treasure" into building that home, I drove by at least once a day. Sometimes I would go by both before and after work. I was excited to see anything; even as boring as a pile of dirt made by the bulldozer. What happened to me? Why was I so enthralled with every step of the construction process? I had invested my treasure in that building process and so my heart had followed my treasure. My heart was deeply passionate about that building process; everything about it became exciting to me. When we invest our treasure in God's kingdom it keeps our heart passionate about the things we should be passionate about. When you give to your local church, you will more deeply care about it. When you give to support missionary work you will be more interested and excited about the souls being reached. Just as Jesus said "Where your treasure is there your heart will be also."

8. Prepare for the fight!

Our last tip on preparing your heart, and keeping it on the right path is found in 1 Peter 5:8 *"Be sober, be vigilant; because your adversary the devil goes about like a roaring lion seeking whom he may devour. Resist him steadfast in the faith."* The amplified translation says "Resist him from the onset."

There have been thousands of wonderful discoveries made throughout history, Einstein and the theory of relativity, the printing press, the combustion engine. But I believe the greatest discovery was made by Enoch. Genesis 5:24 says, *"And Enoch walked with God, and he was not for God took him."* Enoch discovered how to truly walk with God. We must never lose sight of the fact that we can walk with God! It won't happen by accident though. You have to decide ahead of time you are willing to fight for it. Decide ahead of time that you will say "no" to temptation. Don't wait to have a plan until temptation is staring you in the face. You must resist sin and the devil from the onset. Matthew 11:12 says, *"The Kingdom of God suffers violence, and the violent take it by force."*

Don't sit back and think "Well, whatever God wants to happen to me." No, no!! Take the offensive, decide that you will walk with God, that you will please God, and live holy. When you are sitting in front of your television and a program begins that you know you shouldn't watch, change the channel; God isn't going to do it for you. You have got to decide to resist the devil and any temptation he might bring. Psalms 101:3 says, *"I will set nothing wicked before my eyes. I hate the works of those who fall away: it will not cling to me."* Predetermine the choices you will make. Decide

PREDETERMINE THE CHOICES YOU WILL MAKE.

to prepare your heart in each of the eight ways we just discussed. Remember 2 Chronicles 12:14 which says, *"And he did evil because he didn't prepare his heart to seek the Lord."* The implication is clear that if you will prepare your heart, you will do right, you will live a life that is pleasing before God.

AVOIDING POVERTY "LAZINESS"

"Do not carouse with drunkards and gluttons: for they are on their way to poverty and too much sleep clothes a person in rags."

Proverbs 23:19b

In the second part of this verse, Solomon is instructing us how to avoid poverty. Someone might ask "Then why is it talking about friendships and associations again?" The answer is: because one of the biggest factors that will influence your propensity to poverty are your friendships. As humans we have been made for interaction. Most of us realize to be isolated is abnormal. Think of the madman of the Gadarenes. He had 6,000 demons. Scripture tells us he lived alone in tombs. That is classic of Satan's strategy, to try to either isolate or keep you around those who are more spiritually dead than yourself. You were made for community, for family, even the desire within you to belong and be accepted is God given. Solomon says that you must be careful however whom you allow to fulfill that need for community. Satan often attacks by bringing somebody into your life that will bring compromise. Equally, when God desires to bless you, He will often bring people into your life who will strengthen you spiritually.

Proverbs 6:23-24 *"The commandment is a lamp; the law is a light; the reproofs of instruction are the way of life, to keep you from the evil woman."* There is no doubt there are "evil men" out there as well. Notice that God is saying, "I will give you instruction and my Word to keep you from certain people." The famous last words of someone who is led into compromise are, "This relationship won't affect me, I can handle it." The reason 1 Corinthians 15:33 starts with "Do not be deceived" is because God knew that many of us would be. The scripture says *"Do not be deceived, bad company corrupts good morals."*

Solomon, by inspiration from God, is telling us that if we "carouse with drunkards and gluttons" we eventually become one. The good news is that it also works in reverse. Proverbs 13:20 says, *"He who walks with wise men will become wise; a companion of fools will be destroyed."* If you are the smartest person you know, or the most spiritual person you know, you are in big trouble! You need friends that will build you and pull you up.

IF YOU ARE THE SMARTEST PERSON YOU KNOW, OR THE MOST SPIRITUAL PERSON YOU KNOW, YOU ARE IN BIG TROUBLE!

Let's take some time to discuss what poverty is. Proverbs 10:15 says, *"The rich man's wealth is his strong city, but the destruction of the poor is their poverty."* Especially in the "Dark Ages" the concept that poverty was not a curse but in fact a blessing entered into Christianity. Christians began to confuse the love of money with the possession of money. Even today some people confuse greed with financial abundance. The reality is that greed and the love of money are not measured by how much money one has. I have known many people who had very few possessions. Some of them were generous, and others were extremely greedy. They were consumed with a love of money. The fact that they had very little money of their own did not seem to diminish their obsession at all. I have also known many wealthy people and found the same to be true. Some of them were extremely generous with Godly understanding of stewardship and their responsibility to give wisely of what they were given. Then there were others who, even though they had plenty of money, were extremely greedy and consumed with a fear of lack.

Poverty can involve finances but it is not limited to money. High divorce rates among the rich and famous serve as a reminder that many people who are rich in dollars are still poor in their relationships and marriages. Matthew 16:26 puts it this way, *"What does it profit a man to gain the whole world but lose his soul."* I like Derek Prince's definition; he says, "Poverty is having less than all you need to do God's will in your life."

I remember many years ago Jeanie and I had our income tax forms done and the person who filled them out for us looked at what we made and said. "When the government talks about poor people, they are talking about you." Financially that may have been true, but we had a good relationship, we had a good family, we had peace, we had vision, and we didn't consider ourselves impoverished.

Poverty is not a blessing. 3 John 1:2 says, *"Beloved I wish above all things that you would prosper, that you'd be in good health, even as your soul prospers."* This verse states clearly what the life of Abraham also shows us, and that is that biblical prosperity includes far more than finances. It involves health, spiritual well-being; it is an all-encompassing thing. Genesis 24:1 says, *"Now Abraham was old, well advanced in age; and the Lord had blessed Abraham in all things."* Verse 35 lists the silver, gold, and livestock, but that was only a part of the blessing. Abraham was blessed in every possible area.

In 1966, as a nation we officially declared war on poverty. At that time the government said that 14.7% of our population was living in poverty. Now, decades later that number has not decreased, in fact it has increased. The government does not understand that poverty is not a number that you are above or below. It is most often the result of thinking and doing the wrong things. I am not saying every time. But if any person finds themselves consistently or repeatedly impoverished I suggest they compare their actions with God's Word and see if their choices might be a contributing factor.

Here are four things that Proverbs says will bring poverty:

#1 Stinginess: Proverbs 11:24 *"There is one who scatters, yet increases more. There is one who withholds more than is right, but it leads or tends to poverty."* When you do not sow what you should it will bring poverty. Imagine a farmer who was too selfish to plant his seed. No one would be surprised when he didn't have a crop. We are equally ridiculous when we expect blessing to chase us down when we have never planted any seeds of generosity ourselves.

#2 Drunkenness: We are currently looking at Proverbs 23:19 *"Do not carouse with drunkards and gluttons: for they are on their way to poverty"* I didn't say to have a drink is sin, because that isn't what the Bible says. What it does say is that is not wise. There is significant loss of productivity, of health; and alcohol brings turmoil into so many homes. The effect on the children of people who abuse alcohol, or any other addictive substance for that matter, is terrible. Hosea 4:11 says, *"Harlotry, wine, and new wine enslave the heart."* There is so much inherent danger with alcohol, the Bible warns that it will often lead to poverty.

#3 Gluttony: Charismatic Christian culture has been very active in teaching on the biblical dangers of drunkenness and even the abuse of God's temple that smoking is to our body. Somehow it has largely under addressed the issue of gluttony. What is gluttony? The simplest answer is the worship of food or the experience of eating. Most often we think of gluttony as it relates to obesity. A common symptom of gluttony, especially at its extreme, is of course obesity. If someone worships food, in that they allow it to be more important than anything else in their life including health, they will most often gain weight. The problem with using weight as a definition of gluttony is that scripture doesn't say how many pounds equals gluttony. Much like it doesn't assign a dollar amount to greed, or a sentence quota on gossip. As with most sin the key is here in 1 Samuel 16:7 *"The LORD does not look at the things man looks at. Man looks at the outward appearance, but the LORD looks at the heart."* God isn't judging us by the number of holes in our belt or the pounds on our scale. He sees our heart. Have we relinquished the control of our diets to our appetite? Do we surrender to whatever our body craves? Or do we treat our body as the temple of the Holy Ghost, enjoying food but not allowing it to control us? Solomon wisely lists gluttony right next to drunkenness as a path that leads to poverty. Both of those things result from an individual relinquishing the self-control God expects of them and following the cravings of their body instead of wisdom. If you let go of the steering wheel while driving down the road in your car, you will eventually end up in the ditch. Likewise, if you allow your body to steer you instead of steering it, you will eventually suffer harm and most likely find yourself in some form of poverty; financial, relational, health related or perhaps all three.

#4 Laziness: Proverbs 26:13 *"The lazy man says, 'There is a lion in the road! A fierce lion is in the streets!' As a door turns on its hinges, so does the lazy man on his bed. The lazy man is wiser in his own eyes than seven men who can answer sensibly."* John Mason said it this way "Laziness travels so slow that poverty soon overtakes it." Roy Rogers said the same thing a little differently; "Even if you are on the right track you will get run over if you just sit there." When the motivation and wisdom to do what is necessary are lacking, poverty is inevitable.

Those are four things that cause poverty. Now let's look at five steps to blocking poverty. I call them steps because I don't believe that alone any one of these things can inoculate you from poverty. But the combined synergy of these actions together does have the power to break the shackles of poverty.

Five steps to blocking poverty

#1 Be diligent. Proverbs 12:24 *"The hand of the diligent will rule, but the lazy man will be put to forced labor."* I believe that Christians should be the best workers, because we don't work for man, we work for the Lord. The Bible tells you as a Christian, "Don't be an eye-pleaser, don't wait to see if someone is looking." A worker who realizes that they work for God, and that God is always watching, will be very diligent and very thorough.

#2 Be a giver. Proverbs 11:24 *"One man gives freely but grows all the richer; another withholds what he should give and only suffers want."* It may not fit what you learned in first grade about addition and subtraction, but God has His own math. He says those who give generously will grow richer. God's blessing always comes as we give.

#3 Invest for the future. Proverbs 21:20 *"the wise man saves or invests for the future, but the foolish man spends whatever he gets"* I wish I could just reach in and remove bad spending habits for you, I would then replace them with this verse. I had somewhat of an advantage in this area because I grew up in a Dutch home. My family would hardly let an infant out of their crib if they could not balance their checkbook. I remember my grandfather telling me when I was only about seven years old "You never spend more than you make; do you understand that?" I did not even make anything yet, not even an allowance, but he was already drilling that into me.

Proverbs 24:27 *"Prepare your outside work, make it fit for yourself in the field; and afterward build your house;"* There is a principle here that Solomon is trying to convey. He is telling you that before you spend your time and resources on the comforts of home, you should plant your vineyard; make sure you put seed in the ground. When you invest your resources in those things that will yield a return it will sooner be ready to support you. Not just once but a vineyard will continue to pay you back for your efforts year after year after year. First invest in the places that will multiply your investment back to you, then you can afford to go ahead and build your house. The American dream has that sort of back-wards. As Americans we buy our house as soon as we find a lender who will let us, and then we work to try to keep from losing that house. We pay interest to someone else instead of having found a place for our money that would be growing or paying us interest. I wish someone would have told me that when I was twenty, twenty five, or even thirty. Solomon is telling you that you should find and invest in something that will cause your money to work for you.

If I was in charge of your budget, here are the first two things I would do. First off I would tithe. The second thing would be to take the next

GOD WILL BLESS YOUR STOREHOUSE BUT IF YOU DO NOT HAVE ONE, WHAT IS THERE TO BLESS?

10% and invest it. If your reaction is "But I need that to live on," that means you have a habit of spending all that you get. Do you remember what Proverbs 21:20 said? *"The foolish man spends whatever he gets."* If that is you, cheer up! Now you know what you are supposed to do. It may take some time, but if you begin to adjust your habits and implement the self-control God has given you, you can become a saver and investor.

The Bible says that God will bless your storehouse but if you do not have one, what is there to bless? The Bible tells us what percent to tithe, but it doesn't say how much you must invest. It just makes it clear that you should. My recommendation is investing 10%. Malachi 3:10 is a pretty well-known verse. It says that God will open the windows of heaven and pour out a blessing upon you. Let's notice the very next verse Malachi 3:11 *"And I will rebuke the devourer for your sakes, so that he will not destroy the fruit of your ground. Nor shall the vine fail to bear fruit for you in the field, says the Lord of hosts."* What does it say that God will bless? Your vineyard, your orchard, the seed that you have sown for your future. Those are your investments.

I know American culture doesn't celebrate this approach. All I have to say to American culture and anyone who is following it is "If the Bible rubs you the wrong way, it is time to turn around." Solomon said "Prepare your work outside, make it fit for yourself in the field, then build your house."

#4 Rebuke the spirit of poverty and break its power in Jesus' name. Pray for prosperity. Psalms 68:6 says, *"He brings out those who are **bound into prosperity**; But the rebellious dwell in a dry land."* In 2 Samuel chapter 3 there is a story of Joab and how he killed Abner in cold blood. When David hears about it he pronounces a curse on Joab's family in verse 29. *"May his blood fall upon the head of Joab and upon all his father's house! May Joab's house never be without someone who has a running sore or leprosy or who leans on a crutch or who falls by the sword or who lacks food."*

Did you know that a spirit of either prosperity or poverty can be on a person or their family, even for various generations? If you struggle with poverty, I recommend you rebuke it in Jesus' name. Pray the prayer the Psalmist prayed in Psalm 118:25 *"Save, I pray, O Lord; O Lord, I pray , send now prosperity."* If you hadn't prayed for prosperity for fear that it wasn't a Biblical prayer, then pray for it now. It is right there in your instruction manual. Pray that God would prosper you and your family. God wants you to be blessed.

#5 Confess God's favor. Psalms 5:12 says, *"He has surrounded you with favor like a shield."* But you need to do something to activate that favor. Let's look at Ruth. She is living with her mother-in-law Naomi, whose name actually means "the favor of God." However, they are very very poor. Ruth says to Naomi as she is about to leave for the day, "Today, I will go and work in the field of someone in whose eyes I find favor." So before she leaves for work she is saying, "I am going to have favor with my boss today" As the story continues the Bible says she "happens into the part of the field that belongs to Boaz." She confessed that she would have favor. The lowest level of favor is when things happen to work out right; you just happen to be at the right time, to get the right information, to see the right person. Then she finds active favor when Boaz sees her and instructs his workers to intentionally leave handfuls of wheat behind for her to glean. If you study Ruth you will find she experienced increasing levels of favor. So much so that she eventually married Boaz.

Joseph, too, experienced God's favor. He woke up one morning in a dungeon as a prisoner. In the book of Acts it says God gave him wisdom and favor as he went before Pharaoh. That night when he went to bed he was Prime Minister of Egypt! That promotion is about as big as they come. God's favor can open doors that would otherwise be closed. If you want to experience that favor you should do what Ruth did. She confessed it. You should be speaking God's favor over your life saying, "Today I'm going to walk in favor. Today, people will want to hear what I have to say and buy what I have to sell; I am going to have favor in Jesus' name."

CHAPTER 16

VALUE YOUR FAMILY, HONOR YOUR PARENTS, TREASURE YOUR KIDS

"Listen to your father who gave you life and don't despise your mother when she is old. Get wisdom, discipline, and understanding. The father of the righteous will greatly rejoice and he who begets a wise child will delight in him. Let your father and your mother be glad and let her who bore you rejoice."

Proverbs 23:22-25

This is another topic where I especially enjoy getting my wife Jeanie's thoughts since we have parented together for over 39 years, and have been married for even longer. So instead of looking as though I came up with her comments entirely on my own we have decided to tag team this chapter much like we did in chapter 12. This is not to say she hasn't helped with the other chapters because she has. This chapter however is one of those where she has so much to add that is uniquely hers we decided to again change the format so you could more easily distinguish her insights from mine.

Duane:

Let's start as always with the divinely inspired words of Solomon, the wise king. Proverbs 23:22-23 *"Listen to your father who gave you life and don't despise your mother when she is old. Get wisdom, discipline, and understanding. The father of the righteous will greatly rejoice and he who begets a wise child will delight in him. Let your father and your mother be glad and let her who bore you rejoice."*

What does your family mean to you? How do you view your children and your parents, as well as your role as parent and child? Are these things a treasure to you, or have they become a burden, something you dread? That is the topic of Solomon's seventeenth principal for successful living. God clearly desires that we enjoy our children. Psalms 127:3 says *"Sons are a heritage from the Lord. Children are a reward from him."*

Jeanie:

Yes they are a blessing, but that doesn't mean raising children will be without its stressful moments. I remember one night when it seemed I couldn't remember anymore what a good night's rest even felt like. I had been interrupted and interrupted repeatedly. Sometime in the super early hours of morning I looked into the face of my screaming baby and I thought "What is the matter with you?" I just wanted to figure out how to get him to calm down and go back to sleep. I remember thinking to myself, "This is when people abuse their kids." When they come to the end of their rope and they don't have God to hang on to. I remember thinking "God, You are all there is; help me get this right." Difficult moments will come. It is much like a marriage relationship. You need to purposely invest in your marriage and appreciate each other, on purpose choosing to love each other. Many days it will require an "on purpose" decision to love and enjoy your children.

Duane:

The verse opens with "listen to your father." This is speaking to children, which is all of us since everyone is someone's child. Have you ever noticed the more you like someone the easier they are to listen to? No parent is perfect but every child, young and old, has a choice. They can focus on their parent's flaws, which will cause resentment to grow, or focus on their strengths, which will encourage a respectful and honoring relationship. As a child you must purpose to maintain a respectful view of your parents. The command to listen did not include any exceptions for monotone, repetitive, or even short tempered parents. Honoring your parents does not mean believing they are perfect. Especially to an adult child, it means focusing on what they have done right and choosing not to set yourself up as judge over them. It means choosing to treat them only with love.

The wonderful thing about inspired scripture is that it is so profound you can always find more when you take a second look. For example, if children are to listen then what must the parent do? Obviously the parent must instruct. A child can't listen if their parent isn't speaking. As parents you have been entrusted with an eternal soul. Every one of your children are immortal. They have a beginning but will not have an end. No matter what business you are in, the stuff you made or sold will be gone one thousand years from now. But your kids won't be. They will live on someplace forever. As parents we are supposed to do two things; teach and model.

Deuteronomy 6:6 says *"These words which I command you today shall be in your heart."* In order to instruct your children, first God's Word must be in your heart. The verse continues *"and you shall talk of them when you sit in your house, when you walk by the way, when you lie down, when you rise up, you shall bind them as sign on your hand. They shall be as a frontlets between your eyes. You will write them on the door post of your house."* In other words God recommends a fanatical approach to teaching your children. The values, lessons, and morals you want your children to learn need to continuously be in front of them. Put verses on their mirror and inspiring things on your refrigerator door. The Bible is perfectly clear that you are responsible for the instruction of your children. It is not the church's job to teach them about God. Sunday school will help but Sunday school can't take your place.

Jeanie:

One of the ways that we instruct our kids, as well as set the course for our home, is by our example. We should set the example of how to listen to our parents. Our kids shouldn't hear us speak ill of our parents or authority figures. If our kids hear us bad mouthing our parents and grandparents, aunts and uncles, if we constantly go on and on about how stupid they are, and how worthless their advice is, how can we expect our kids to respect and appreciate us? We are teaching them to only respect people with whom you agree, and not showing them that we are to be respectful of the position they hold. They will learn the value of family by watching us. I recently read in my journal this story that took place when our son Daniel was very young. Duane had recently begun to focus on the importance of being appreciative. He would compliment me or the food I prepared regularly. Duane didn't sit Daniel down and tell him what to do or what to say. But it was only about three days later that I wrote down these comments that came from Daniel who was about seven years old "Mom, you sure know the way to a man's heart." "This food is so good. You are the best cook in the world and I'm not just saying that to pass the time." It is so amazing to see how naturally they pick up our behavior, even changes in our behavior.

Duane:

Genesis 18:19 is speaking about Abraham whom God chose to be the father of our faith. It says *"For I have known him in order that he may command his children and his household **after him**, that they may keep the way of the Lord to do righteousness and justice, that the Lord may bring to Abraham what he spoke to him."* Notice how God said He would command his household after him. This means he will not live one way yet instruct his family to do something else. It may not popular in today's culture but it also says he commanded his family.

I have been far too frequently surprised by Christians who say to their 12 year old children "Do you want to go do church or not?" You don't ask them. You should tell them. You make choices and when you make right choices for them you teach them to make right choices for themselves. Deuteronomy 30:19 is an excellent example of the trickle-down effect of decision making. It says *"I called heaven and earth as a witness today against you, for I set before you life and death, blessing and cursing. Therefore, choose life, that both you and your descendants may live."*

Have you ever seen a behavior in your parents and said to yourself "I will never do that," only to find yourself doing it? Jude 1:10 talks about "the things that they knew 'naturally' destroyed them." Perhaps no one ever actually tried to convince you it is the right thing to do to raise your voice and shout when you really want to win an argument, but if that is what you saw over and over as you grew up then it just feels natural. That is why we so often find ourselves gravitating to the behavior of our parents, even the behaviors we didn't want to imitate. If we haven't replaced what we have always experienced with a clear image of what scripture shows us we should do, we will gravitate to what we know the best by default. That is why it is important to fill yourself with scripture. When you know scripture more intimately than you know the memories of how you were raised your parenting will no longer naturally follow your experience.

Notice what Solomon said in verse 25 of chapter 23, which is the saying we are studying here. *"Let your father and your mother be glad and let her who bore you rejoice."* God is telling us through Solomon that we should put a very, very high value on our children, on our family, and our relationships. Our family should be a source of joy for us. Have you ever heard of a person on their death bed saying "I wish I could take my luxury car for one more drive?" or "I would like to count my money one last time." Of course not, that isn't what life is about. Unfortunately many people don't realize that

until it's too late. Everyone understands immediately when faced
with death what Solomon is trying to get us to notice while we still
have time to act on it. Enjoy your family, enjoy your kids, and don't
ignore your parents as they age. (verse 22 said *"do not despise your
mother when she is old."*)

Solomon left several keys to an enduringly happy family right
here. He is showing us how to be a family that enjoys each other
and avoids unnecessary offense or neglect. He said for the children
to listen and the adults to teach. Proverbs is loaded with advice for
parents and children alike on how to teach and listen, how to correct,
and how to respect.

God designed us for fellowship. He is reminding us that your
greatest joys should come from your family. Not from things, but from
people. Our culture has lost sight of that truth. Statistically, people are
waiting longer and longer to marry, and having fewer and fewer children. I believe it is partly because our culture has increasingly looked
to money, to things, to experiences and entertainment to bring them
the joy that God intended our family and relationships to bring.

Jeanie:

I want to share with you a tool that has been very effective in helping me to truly enjoy our family. It is my journal. I know some people feel journaling is a place to vent your frustrations and to give a
voice to the things that upset you, to articulate and immortalize your
resentments. I don't think those journals are helping anyone. That
isn't the kind of journal I keep. Philippians 4:8 says *"Finally, brothers,
whatever is true, whatever is noble, whatever is right, whatever is pure,
whatever is lovely, whatever is admirable—if anything is excellent or
praiseworthy—think about such things."*

I already shared with you that raising a family wasn't always
a cake walk. But I want to plant a seed in you, especially if you are
a new parent. Take the time to write down the special moments.
When we began our family we lived on the mission field, before
the Internet and cell phones. When one of our kids would say or

do something funny or cute I would write it down, so that I could remember to tell Duane when he got home and so I could include it in my letters back to the USA. I still have a box filled with napkins, the backs of envelopes, and the backs of receipts where I wrote cute and clever things the kids did. It really is fun to raise a family. These memories, and the ability to pick them up and relive those wonderful moments, have inspired me many times.

I want to share some of those moments with you both because as a mother I enjoy talking about my kids but also because I hope it can inspire you to find a way to focus on the positive side of your family. In our home hunting was always a big deal. Our son Daniel, when he was maybe six years old, was talking to Duane's assistant Norma, and she said she liked chicken. He quickly responded "Well then when it is chicken season I will get you some." When our oldest son, Joshua, was only three years old he smashed his finger and because he didn't know what to call his fingernail he said "Mom, I hurt the plastic part of my finger."

You can learn about logic by listening to young kids. They say things that may be wrong but they sure make a lot of sense. Another time Josh came inside after he had cut his elbow and said "Oh Mom, I am painting!" His arm was bleeding what to him looked almost like red paint. On another occasion I walked into our kitchen to find a broken jar and the contents spilled everywhere, I said "Ah, who did this? What a happened here?" Our daughter Stephanie's little eyes got real big and she said "Maybe I did it. No, I better not say that because it has the words 'I did it' in it and I don't like to say that." Since we have four children I will attempt to give them each a story so I will give you one more. Josh was describing the idealistic scene he had recently witnessed of a couple sitting in front of an old black and white movie while the father sat in his recliner with a newspaper and the mother was darning. Samuel who was perhaps 12 or 13 at the time said, "What is darning?" Josh replied "Oh, it is a kind of sewing." "Oooh" Samuel replied as his expression changed "I thought she was sitting there saying darn, darn, darn, darn...."

Enjoy your kids, enjoy your parents, don't sweat the small stuff. Decide that every offense is small stuff when weighed against the alternative of a life cut off from the relationships that are designed to bring us joy.

Duane:

Many of you are parents, and to you I say that raising your kids will be one of the most important things that you do. I want to encourage you that it will be well worth the time and effort to raise them according to scripture. Be a radical parent, fill your heart with God's Word and then let it overflow onto your kids. Honor your parents for this is right. Remember, you were made in God's image for relationship with Him and with others. Without those relationships you will not find true happiness.

DECIDE THAT EVERY OFFENSE IS SMALL STUFF WHEN WEIGHED AGAINST THE ALTERNATIVE OF A LIFE CUT OFF FROM THE RELATIONSHIPS THAT ARE DESIGNED TO BRING US JOY.

Jeanie:

I want to close this chapter with this thought. I realize that sometimes when your heart is full of hurts, mistakes that maybe your parents made, resentments, bitterness, anger, any number of things, all you are able to do is react out of that hurt. Instead of being able to respond out of a heart that is strong and secure, forgiven and washed clean, it may feel impossible to enjoy life. God is the one who can cleanse you of those things and heal your heart. Jesus came to heal the broken hearted. Nothing that was done to you was so bad that God cannot heal it. God loves you and wants to heal the hurt in your heart so that you can be free to enjoy your family.

CHAPTER 17

IMMORALITY– PORNOGRAPHY

"Pay close attention, son, and let my life be your example. Prostitutes and immoral women are a deadly trap. They wait for you like robbers and cause many men to be unfaithful."

Proverbs 23:26-28 GNT

In the New American Standard version this verse says *"Give me your heart, son, and let your eyes delight in my ways. For a harlot is a deep pit and an adulterous woman a narrow well. Surely she lurks as a robber and increases the faithless among men."*

As we begin this saying, I think it is important to remember that the Bible is not a list of don'ts and bunch of rules to follow. It is God's guide to knowing Him and living the most fulfilling life possible. When He says something is a deadly trap it is because it is. Most Christians who ignore the biblical standards of morality especially in the area of sex don't do it because they are ignorant of what God says. They make ungodly choices because they believe they know better than God what will bring them happiness. They are hoping to taste sin often, even with a plan to repent and go back to righteous living before the consequences catch up with them. So right now I want to settle in your mind that everything God tells us He says because He wants you to have the best life possible.

God calls it a trap and a pit because it works just like a trap; it looks far safer from the outside than it really is. The Bible says about sin that, *"It will not deliver or release those who give themselves to it."* Proverbs 5:22 says, *"His own iniquity entraps the wicked man and he's caught in the cords of sin."* In other words sin has tentacles and it grabs you. You may think "I am just going to be here for a moment. Then I will go back to the straight and narrow." But when you try to leave there is that tentacle, that cord it is around your leg and it just keeps yanking you back. The Bible describes it as a deep pit. I like to describe sin like this; sin keeps you longer than you wanted to stay, costs you more than you wanted to pay, and pulls you further than expected away.

Hosea 4:11 says *"Harlotry, wine, and new wine enslave the heart."* In today's language instead of harlotry we would say prostitution, fornication, adultery, and pornography. In fact, in our internet inundated world I believe the number one danger is pornography. Don't let anyone soften the seriousness and danger of these sins. The Bible calls them a pit or a trap. I want everyone reading this book to be a better prepared individual. Be aware that it will enslave your heart away from God, away from your spouse, and away from your family. To help bring home the seriousness of this problem in our culture allow me to quote some statistics I was given a few years ago…

There are over 4.2 million pornography sites on the Internet. That is 12% of all websites. Daily search engine requests are 68 million and 25% of them request pornography. Daily pornographic emails are about 2.5 billion, which is 8% of all emails. The average age of first Internet exposure to pornography is 11 years old. When a large group of 8-16 year old children were asked if they had viewed porn on line while doing homework, 90% answered yes. If you are thinking that these numbers only reflect non-Christians, at a Promise Keepers event a few years ago, which consists of Christian men, the good guys who want to do what is right, 53% said they had viewed pornography in the last week.

Just like the verse said it is a trap. If your spouse or child is caught in it, the temptation will be to get mad. And if it is your spouse I can see why, because it is very hurtful. But what they need is love, and a lot of help. Much of the power of these secret sins comes from the fear of negative reactions. Those who are struggling need friends who will love them yet hate the sin. Your spouse or child needs to know that the sin is 100% unacceptable but that you still love and accept them, just as God never accepted sin but always accepted us. It is a powerful thing when two Christians take godliness seriously and are no longer afraid to be open about their own temptations and hold each other accountable to a zero tolerance for compromise.

This is no minor issue, and it isn't just a problem that spiritual "losers" have. Look at your Bible. David was God's best man and he fell into sexual sin. Sampson was God's strongest man and he fell into sexual sin. Solomon was God's wisest man and even he messed up sexually. If God's wisest, strongest, and best all had to face it, most of us may also be tempted.

2 Timothy 2:22 says *"Flee also youthful lust but pursue righteousness."* It is not just deciding what you won't do. You have to pursue righteousness, faith, love, and peace. Plans that simply involve the will power to quit doing wrong have a poor chance of success. God says you need to not just flee what is wrong but also pursue what is right.

Somehow the church, in an attempt to not be crass, has stopped talking about sex all together. It doesn't talk about sexual sin except to quickly say it is bad. It definitely does not talk about what a Godly sexual relationship is or requires. As a result, when our young, or old people for that matter, are faced with an opportunity to engage in sexual compromise (which is sin), they can't think of a good reason to say no. They easily fall into the trap of thinking "I am just going to do this for a little while." But the truth is that sin is a pit, it is a trap, and you get a cord of sin around you. Sin keeps you longer than you wanted to stay, costs you more than you wanted to pay, and pulls you further than expected away.

Pornography does not satisfy. It increases and increases a lust inside of a person. It is like taking a drink that you expect will quench your thirst but instead it makes you thirstier and thirstier with every gulp. It is a perversion and bondage. It creates an appetite that normal sex will not satisfy. Sadly, many people come to a point where they prefer pornography to normal sex. One sex addict said "I have had to face the sad fact that for me sex has become fun to watch, exciting to think about, but completely unfulfilling to engage in."

SIN KEEPS YOU LONGER THAN YOU WANTED TO STAY, COSTS YOU MORE THAN YOU WANTED TO PAY, AND PULLS YOU FURTHER THAN EXPECTED AWAY.

Over 30 years ago when I first began pastoring, I spoke with a man who was at that time already 60 years old, if not older. This is the story he told me. "At the end of World War II, I was stationed in France, right outside of Paris. A group of young guys and I went into town. I was a virgin until that night when I spent the evening with a prostitute. I didn't think much of it at that time. I returned from the war, I fell in love, and I got married. But it was the strangest thing, Pastor, every time I was with my wife I thought of that woman. Every time I was together sexually with my wife I couldn't shake the thoughts of that prostitute, every time! It caused so much turmoil eventually we got divorced. I was single for several years and I eventually remarried." I could see in his face and hear in his voice the despair and frustration this had caused him. As this grown man emotionally broke down he said "Now the exact thing is happening again!" Do you realize he was telling me about something that had happened over 40 years ago? Ezekiel 23:21 says, *"thus she called to remembrance the lewdness of her youth."* How this man wished some-one had warned him about the dangers of sin.

Thousands of single young men and women have thought that the appetite for pornography or promiscuity they developed while single would be satisfied by their spouse within marriage. Sadly, they are surprised to find that what they convinced themselves was an appetite for normal sex when they were single is actually a lust for sin that was created by their compromise, and it is unquenched by their marriage. This is not because their marriage is insufficient in any way! It is because sin does not create a desire for something healthy. It births lust which will not be satisfied even by the behavior it craves, much less by something healthy. To kill lust you must follow scripture, "flee youthful lusts," repent and renounce it, cut off every inappropriate source of lustful stimuli. Pray and ask for God's help. You have to quit cold turkey while pursuing righteousness.

We need to wake up and realize that our culture and Hollywood are selling us a lie. The truth is that if one man marries one woman and they are faithful to each other for life, they will have the best sex. Those two people will experience the most fulfillment, because they are following the designer's instructions. Hollywood is right about only one thing; sex is wonderful! God designed it to be extremely enjoyable and unifying and special. The problem Hollywood has is they are totally wrong about how to best experience the joys God intended sex to bring. They will sell you everything but the right answer. Acts 2:40 is the sermon that gave birth to the church. Peter said *"Be saved from this perverse generation."* Do you realize he didn't say "be saved from hell," or "be saved from sin." That is as true today as it was then. We live in a perverse generation and we must be saved from it. We must be different than the world we live in.

1 Corinthians chapter 7 the first few verses in the Message translation are extremely clear. It says *"It's good for a man to have a wife and for a woman to have a husband. Sexual drives are strong, but marriage is strong enough to contain them and provide for a balanced and fulfilling sexual life in a world of sexual disorder. The marriage bed must be a place of mutuality; the husband seeking to satisfy his wife and the wife seeking*

to satisfy her husband. Marriage is not a place to stand up for your rights. Marriage is a decision to serve the other whether in bed or out. Abstaining from sex is permissible for a period of time if you both agree to it. And if it's for the purposes of prayer and fasting—but only for such times. Then come back together again. Satan has an ingenious way of tempting us when we least expect it. I'm not, understand, commanding these periods of absti- nence—only providing my best counsel if you should choose them."

That wasn't my opinion that was scripture. Let's revisit what it said. Marriage is great and so is sex, and it is designed to be the unself- ish, shared giving of each other to each other for mutual enjoyment. Then it says if a married couple wants to abstain from sex that it can be acceptable only if it is for a short period of time and only to pray and fast. If you wonder how long it is biblical for a married couple to abstain from physical intimacy, the answer is: how long can you fast? And it also says this should be a decision you agree upon. That means abstinence is not to be used as a punishment or manipulation.

Before you are married Satan will do everything he can to get you to have sex, and as soon as you get married he will try to keep you apart. I recently spoke with a pastor who worked as a marriage counselor. He told me how couples would come to him who hadn't had sex for a year, two years, five years, even ten! Let me straighten something out here. If you think you are too spiritual for sex you are flaky. Enoch walked with God and he had sons and daughters during that time. Sex inside of marriage will draw you closer to each other and is pleasing to God Who created it. Yes, God created sex. Not Hugh Hefner, not Hollywood; we need to stop allowing the world to steal sex. God created it for pleasure. He made it in the beginning and He said it was good and wonderful and holy. Satan, through pornography and casual sex outside of marriage, tries to undermine that. He tries to make sex look like something casual and nonexclusive. He wants to convince us that what we do with our bodies is unimportant. But you are the temple of the Holy Ghost. God redeemed you spirit, soul and body.

CHAPTER 18

AVOIDING DRUNKENNESS– THE EFFECTS AND DANGERS OF ALCOHOL

"Who has woe? Who has sorrow? Who has contentions? Who has complaints? Who has wounds without cause? Who has redness of eyes? Those who linger long over wine, those who go in search of mixed wine. Don't look at the wine when it's red and sparkles in the cup, when it swirls around smoothly. At the last it bites like a serpent and stings like a viper. Your eyes will see strange things, and your heart will utter perverse things. Yes, you will be like one who lies down in the midst of the sea, like one who lies on the top of a mast. They struck me, but I was not hurt. They have beaten me, but I didn't feel it. When shall I awake? I will seek another drink."

Proverbs 23:29-35

Alcohol is a topic that does not get preached on very frequently. I understand pastors hesitation to bring it up since it will undoubtedly ruffle some feathers. But as you can see it is not a topic that the Bible is silent about. As we dive into this subject I want to make one thing clear from the beginning. I do not believe that it is a sin to drink a beer or to have a cup of wine. I believe "social drinking" as it is called to not be sin in every instance. I do not, however, consider it to be wise either.

Let's look again at Solomon's description of the effects of wine, this time from the Message translation. Proverbs 23: 29-35 *"Who are the people who are always crying the blues? Who do you know who reeks of self-pity? Who keeps getting beat up for no reason at all? Whose eyes are blurry and bloodshot? It's those who spend the night with the bottle, for whom drinking is serious business. Don't judge wine by its label or by its bouquet for its full bodied flavor. Judge it rather by the hangover it leaves you with. The splitting headache. The queasy stomach. Do you really prefer seeing double? With your speech all slurred, reeling, and seasick? Drunk as a sailor? They hit me you'll say, but it didn't hurt. They beat me, but I didn't feel a thing. When I'm sober enough to manage it, bring me another drink."*

Some people reading this will hear the part where I say "You can have a beer without being in sin" and think to themselves "What a relief, I really didn't want to hear anything that would require me to change." If that thought went through your mind on this chapter, any other chapter of this book, or any Bible teaching, I want to encourage you; in fact I dare you to read the Bible and teachings from the Bible. Not to ensure that you are still getting into heaven, but to see how you might improve yourself for God's glory even more. An athlete does not run a race and say "Phew, I am just happy I am still at least average." No even when he has done his best ever he goes to his coach and says "What can I do to improve?

God does not look at alcohol or any of our behavior through the lens of our culture and what is or is not widely acceptable. He looks objectively through the lens of truth and His word. Let's forget whether we like the taste or not and take a look at some objective statistics about alcohol. 55% of people in the United States over 12 years old used alcohol in the last 30 days. The per capita yearly consumption of beer in our nation is 56 gallons. One in four families suffers from alcohol related problems. That is a lot! There are over 14 million alcoholics in the United States, and those 14 million drink 51% of the alcohol consumed. Alcohol is a factor in one half of all highway deaths. One half of all murders involve alcohol. 69% of all drownings, 70% of all fatal falls, 83% of all deaths in fire, 47% of all industrial accidents, 50% of all arrests, 50% of all rapes, 69% of all child abuse and the list goes on.

1 Corinthians 6:9-10 says, *"Do you not know that the unrighteous will not inherit the kingdom of God. Do not be deceived neither fornicators, nor idolaters, nor adulterers, nor homosexuals, nor sodomites, nor thieves, nor covetous, nor drunkards, nor revilers, nor extortionists will enter or inherit the kingdom of God."*

Our culture not only accepts drunkenness, it often glorifies it. The Bible clearly says "drunkards go to hell." Those are harsh words, especially for something our worldly culture considers fun. But God doesn't judge us based on culture He judges us according to His word. As I said earlier there is no scripture that says having a drink is sin, but now we see that getting drunk is sin according to scripture.

As a teacher I spend most of my time telling you what I know. Let me take a second to tell you something I don't know. I do not know how many times you need to get drunk to be considered a drunkard. Is it 12 times a year, six times a year, three times? We usually call someone who kills even once a killer, but a drunkard, I don't know.

In America we typically call people who have problems with alcohol, alcoholics, and we say they have a disease. God will not send anybody to hell for having any disease. If alcoholism is a disease it is the only one that we bottle, sell, and advertise. So for that reason I won't use the term alcoholic. I will stick the biblical term drunkard.

The verse following that list of people who will not inherit the kingdom of God says "and such were some of you but you were washed you were sanctified, and you were justified in the name of the Lord Jesus Christ and by the Spirit of our God" (1 Corinthians 6:11). Some of the Christians to whom Paul is writing were adulterers, fornicators, homosexuals, thieves, covetous, drunkards, and extortionists, but they repented and were forgiven.

Here are five things that drunkenness does:

1. Brings a curse on your family. In Genesis chapter 9 we find the very first scriptural mention of drunkenness. It is after the flood. Noah has planted a vineyard and he got drunk off the wine. He ends up naked in his tent. Lewdness and alcohol go together. Verses 22-25 say, *"Ham, the father of Canaan, saw the nakedness of their father, and he told his two brothers outside. Shem and Japheth took a garment and laid it on both their shoulders, and went backward and covered the nakedness of their father. So when Noah awoke from his wine and knew what younger son had done to him. Then he said: "Cursed be Canaan. A servant of servants he shall be to his brethren."*

Notice that Ham is the one who did wrong but Noah cursed Canaan, who was Ham's son. Ham is accountable for his own actions but his actions still brought a curse on his family. Penitentiaries are filled with thousands of young men who committed crimes and are therefore responsible for those crimes, but the root cause is a father who was a drunkard. When a person becomes addicted to a substance be it alcohol or drugs, the decisions they make are increasingly made by the addiction. Where they go, what they do, how they spend the family's money. As a result they cannot give love, or receive it properly. In the end children get abused, wives are beaten, money is wasted, hopes are destroyed, and lives are crippled by the addiction, by drunkenness. The pain is often worse for the family than individual. The curse of alcoholism falls on the family.

2. Alcohol will enslave your heart. Hosea 4:11 *"Harlotry, wine, and new wine enslave the heart."* This verse is saying that wine will enslave your heart. It will take it where you didn't want it to go. It will demand more and more of your heart for itself until it no longer belongs to God, or your spouse, or your kids. It will enslave your heart until wine becomes its singular passion. The more you give of yourself to wine (alcohol), the more alcohol can enslave you away from God, your spouse, and your family.

3. Drunkenness causes even the righteous to act shamefully. In Genesis there's a story about a man named Lot. In 2 Peter 2:11 it says *"God delivered righteous Lot who was oppressed by the filthy conduct of the wicked."* Lot had been living for a number of years in the city of Sodom and he had remained righteous in spite of the intense wickedness of the city. All that time he had withstood the pressure of the evil that was there. But what the horrible influences of Sodom and Gomorrah had not been able to accomplish his two daughters with the help of some wine did. Lot had escaped the destruction of Sodom and Gomorrah with only his two daughters. Perhaps you recall that his wife had been turned into a pillar of salt because she turned back. Scripture tells us how the daughters said to each other *"Come, let us make our father drink wine and we will lie with him so that we can preserve the lineage of our father."* So they made their father drink wine and that night the first born went in and lie with her father, and he didn't know when she lie down or when she arose. After all those years of resisting wickedness Lot committed incest after getting drunk. This is another example of how lewdness and drunkenness go hand in hand. Was he responsible for his actions, even though he was so drunk? Absolutely he was responsible. He chose to get drunk so he was responsible. We have no excuse for not realizing what drunkenness does. Habakkuk 2:15 says, *"Woe to him who gives drink to his neighbor pressing into your bottle even to make him drunk that you may look on his nakedness. You are filled with shame instead of glory."* Notice again the connection between drunkenness and lewdness, even immorality.

4. Drunkenness tends to poverty. Proverbs 23:21 states, *"For the drunkard and the glutton will come to poverty."* Whose mission statement lines up with the effects of drunkenness? John 10:10 says *"The thief comes only to steal and kill and destroy; I have come that they may have life, and have it to the full."* When you take what God has blessed you with and use it to get drunk it opens a door for the enemy to come in and attack your family, finances, health, and good name.

5. It produces bondage. Proverbs 5:1 *"Wine is a mocker, strong drink a brawler, and whoever is led astray by it is not wise."* I want you to have a good life, a strong family. One of Satan's strongest allies has been alcohol. Perhaps you take a drink now and again and have things under control. That is great, I am glad to hear it. Just know that Satan will be trying to push you over that ledge as long as it is anywhere nearby.

Here are the four biggest reasons why I believe that even though drinking is not a sin you and I should still choose not to drink.

1. We need to take a righteous stand against a satanic attack.
It is clear that alcohol is a weapon in Satan's arsenal. Why support one of his most successful tools?

2. I believe it compromises your testimony.
1 Thessalonians 5:22 says *"Abstain from all appearance of evil."* God asks us to avoid even looking like we may be sinning.

3. It causes your weak brother to stumble.
Romans 14:21 *"It is better not to eat meat or drink wine or to do anything else that will cause your brother to fall."*

4. As Christians we should set a godly example for our kids.
Prov 22:6 says, *"Train up a child in the way he should go, and when he is old he will not turn from it."* Perhaps you say "I don't have a problem restraining myself." How about your kids, are you sure that they all will be equally able to walk up to the edge without falling?

As I close this chapter I want to address the most famous scriptural argument for drinking. When desiring to defend alcohol consumption people will say "Well it must be alright because Jesus' first miracle was turning water into wine." First let me point out that no matter what sort of wine his miracle produced it in no way changes any of the previously mentioned four reasons why I don't drink nor does it negate the five things we saw that drunkenness does. Personally, when I look at everything the Bible says about drunkenness and knowing that Jesus came to fulfill scripture not to abolish it and to bring life not take it, I find it surprising that Jesus' first miracle would be to aid in getting a large crowd drunk. In Bible times the word wine was used for any drink made of grape, both intoxicating and not. Before refrigerators, storing food and drink was a lot harder than it is now. A common practice in Jesus' day was to take what we would call wine, which is grape juice that may have begun to ferment, and boil it until it had thickened. They would boil at least half of the water out of it. Of course boiling takes place at 212 degrees. Yeast, which is the ingredient that makes alcohol, is destroyed at 170 degrees. So what is left would be sort of like grape juice concentrate. They could take that "wine" and store it in wine skins for months or even years and then just add water whenever they were ready to serve it. I personally believe it was a wine like that which was not capable of making the guests drunk that Jesus made. However, even if I assume that Jesus made a chardonnay from that water everything that scripture says still stands. Alcohol has some very dangerous tendencies. Drunkenness is a sin. And anyone who desires to "drink socially" should do so with extreme caution.

CHAPTER 19

THE IMPORTANCE OF CHOOSING FRIENDS

"Don't envy wicked men and don't desire their company for their heart plots violence and their lips talk of making trouble."

Proverbs 24:1

Look closely at why Solomon says that you should not desire the company of wicked men. He didn't say it was because of the evil things they are doing. This scripture says it is because of what they think, and what they say. In addition to addressing their thoughts, when he tells us to not envy he is telling us to watch what we think. Envy is a thought process. Envy involves you seeing someone else's life or possessions and thinking intently about how much you wish that life or those things were yours. It is a form of meditation. Eastern religions talk a lot about meditation but that is actually a very different kind of meditation than Biblical meditation. In most eastern religions the goal of meditation is to empty your mind of thoughts. They will attempt to repeat a meaningless mantra until they can stop thinking about anything at all. They believe that brings them closer to the peaceful nothingness they call heaven or Nirvana.

Biblical meditation is not about emptying your mind but about filling it up. We should meditate on God's Word in order to be filled with its truth and power. Envy is a form of meditating but on something inappropriate.

Why do the thoughts and speech of our friends matter so much? Why didn't God say we could have any friendship we would like as long as we don't commit any sins with those who commit them? Of course the answer is because God knows us even better than we know ourselves.

In Matthew 12:35 Jesus said, *"A good man out of the good treasure of his heart brings forth good things and an evil man out of the evil treasure brings forth evil things."* God knows that no matter what your intentions are to begin with, you will ultimately move

NO MATTER WHAT YOUR INTENTIONS ARE TO BEGIN WITH, YOU WILL ULTIMATELY MOVE IN THE DIRECTION OF YOUR DOMINANT THOUGHT

in the direction of your dominant thought. We looked at the story of Elijah a few chapters ago. How even after experiencing a chain of incredible successes he dwelled on Jezebel's threats against his life and became suicidal.

Today's thoughts are tomorrow's actions. Today's bigotry is tomorrow's prejudice. Today's lust is tomorrow's adultery. Today's greed is tomorrow's embezzlement. Jeremiah 6:9 says, *"I will certainly bring calamity on this people, the fruit of their thoughts, because they have not heeded My words."* Have you ever noticed how the things you think on will grow just like a farmer's seeds will grow in the ground? Jesus said in Matthew 12:33, *"Either make the tree good and its fruit good, or else make the tree bad and its fruit bad; for a tree is known by its fruit."* Jesus isn't talking about trees of course. He is talking about people. A tree doesn't change but people do. The tree is your heart. If you make your heart good you will produce good fruit.

If you make your heart bad, you will produce bad fruit. So what will determine the direction for your heart? Your thoughts will direct your heart. The things you meditate on will determine the nature of your heart which in turn determines the fruit of your life. And who chooses your thoughts? You do.

Proverbs 12:26 says, *"The righteous chooses his friends carefully. For the way of the wicked leads them astray."* The people around us and their conversations as well as our surroundings all have an effect on us. This is especially true for those we allow into our inner circles whether we like to admit it or not. 1 Corinthians 15:33 says famously, *"Don't be deceived, evil company corrupts good habits or good morals."*

Several years ago I met with a business man who had just returned from a very celebrated seminar. I was anxious to try and glean some wisdom from him so I asked "tell me, what are some predominant things you picked up? Is there anything that really stood out to you?" He responded that "the speaker told us 'If you wrote down the names of your five closest associates and friends and then put their yearly incomes beside their names, the average of those incomes would be your income.' So I tried it and it worked!" The same principle that Solomon is talking about the seminar speaker had applied to the financial realm. I don't know for sure how precise that financial example really is but I know that scripture is right on when it says *"bad company corrupts good morals."* It is often interesting how unaware we are of the influences of our friends but that doesn't diminish the effect any.

Haggai 2:12 says, *"If one carries holy meat in the fold of his garment, and with edge he touches bread or stew, wine or oil, or any food, will it become holy?"* Then the priests answered and said "No" and Haggai said, "If one who is unclean because of a dead body touches any of these will it be unclean?" So the priests answered and said "It shall be unclean." The principle here is that it is much easier for something unclean to contaminate that which is clean than for the something clean to purify something unclean. 1 Corinthians 15:13 didn't say "good company improves bad morals."

1 Corinthians 5: 9-11 says, *"I have written you in my letter not to associate with sexually immoral people—not at all meaning the people of this world who are immoral, or the greedy and swindlers, or idolaters. In that case you would have to leave this world. But now I am writing you that you must not associate with anyone who calls himself a brother but is sexually immoral or greedy, an idolater or a slanderer, a drunkard or a swindler. With such a man do not even eat."* Let's close this chapter by applying this to our own lives. If I am going to follow Biblical advice who will my friends be? First, your closest friends will be people whom you have carefully selected in order to avoid hypocrisy and sin. For your outer circles of friendship you may carefully include people of the world for it is by observing the love you show for your fellow Christians that they will come to know God. But anyone who claims to be a righteous Christian yet excuses sin in their life, or anyone who would say or attempt to imply that the sin in their life is acceptable don't even eat with them.

CHAPTER 20

UNDERSTANDING WISDOM AND KNOWLEDGE

"By wisdom a house is built, and by understanding it is established, by knowledge the rooms are filled with rare and beautiful treasures." (NIV)

"Any enterprise is built by wise planning, becomes strong through common sense, and profits wonderfully by keeping abreast of the facts." (LB)

Proverbs 24:3

In this saying Solomon is giving us a powerful recipe. Notice the three ingredients; wisdom, understanding, and knowledge. These three things, when combined and applied to an endeavor, have a synergy that is nearly unstoppable. Each by themselves are helpful but when combined Solomon says the results will be like beautiful treasures.

You have undoubtedly seen situations where only one ingredient was at work without the others. Often people scratch their heads and say, "It is so strange that this person is not experiencing more success. They seem to have a lot going for them." I have seen many a pastor with the wisdom to start a church reach a certain point and just plateau indefinitely. They don't have an understanding of what to do to take it to another level. Let's take a look at these three ingredients.

By wisdom, the scripture says, a house is built. Proverbs 14:1 similarly says *"a wise woman builds her house."* To build you need wisdom. Wisdom is the ability to see the probable outcomes of any given choice. True wisdom will always choose God's way because it foresees the dangers and consequences of sin and compromise.

TRUE WISDOM WILL ALWAYS CHOOSE GOD'S WAY BECAUSE IT FORESEES THE DANGERS AND CONSEQUENCES OF SIN AND COMPROMISE.

Wisdom is quite possibly one of the most powerful forces on earth. It is the difference between prosperity and poverty, between decrease and increase, between loss and gain. That is why Solomon says in Proverbs 4:7 *"wisdom is the principle thing. Therefore get wisdom. And in all your getting get understanding."*

Understanding is something that is established, whether it is in your marriage or your business, it thrives, it flourishes, it grows, it succeeds. It doesn't just plateau but it keeps on going to new levels. I believe an excellent example is the kingdom of Israel under David and then Solomon. Each reigned for forty years. Together they represent 80 years of very effective leadership. Israel thrived under those two kings. The stability and prosperity that Israel attained during their rule has literally never been matched. After Solomon's death, however, the benefits of the incredible leadership, all the wisdom and understanding, were thrown away within 30 days. Solomon's son Rehoboam becomes king and the people come and say "Rehoboam, look at what has happened. Under your father, taxes were high and impressive things were accomplished, but we want things to get better." He sends them away and takes three days to speak with his father's counselors who tell him he needs to serve the people. "If you answer them kindly from the beginning and show them you will understand their needs, they will in turn be your servants forever." But then he went and talked to some young people. Their advice was to show them who was boss. So he followed the advice of his inexperienced friends and told Israel *"If my father taxed you a little I will tax you a lot. My father punished you with whips; I'm going to punish you with scorpions. My little finger is thicker than my father's waist."* (1 Kings 12:10) They got his message but it didn't work like he had hoped. Ten of the 12 tribes of Israel left; the nation was split in two. Israel never again reached the glory of David and Solomon's reign. How was Rehahoam able to destroy in 30 days what took 80 years to build? It was because he didn't have understanding. Things will not continue to grow, to thrive, and to succeed without understanding. This is true of your business as well as your marriage. Husbands if you make it your business to understand your wife's needs your marriage will thrive, it will be strong.

Thirdly, Solomon says that you need to have knowledge, or as the Living Bible put it, keep abreast of the facts. So now that you are wise enough to choose the right road, you need to have the understanding to know how to continue down the road. You learn what is around you on the road. What do the people here expect of you? Once you know what is expected then it is time to exceed that.

I like to call it the Rebekah Principle. Abraham's son was nearly 40 years old and not married so Abraham sends his servant Eleazar several hundred miles back to the land of Abraham's ancestors and family to find Isaac a wife. Most kids today seem to hardly trust their parents to give advice about selecting a wife let alone allowing their parents to delegate the job to one of their employees. But that is what Abraham did and it worked very well for them. Eleazar, as he is approaching the place he was sent, prays and asks God to show him the woman he is to choose. He asks that she offer not only him a drink but also give his ten camels all the water they need also. He sees Rebekah approach the well and asks for a drink. She proceeds to say that she will also water the camels until they are satisfied. Most of us don't realize what a huge thing that is. A thirsty camel drinks between 30-40 gallons of water and Eleazar had ten camels! She didn't have a faucet, she would have to lower a bucket and then raise it for each gallon or two. This took probably a good two hours and a lot of hard work. She wasn't chosen for her beauty, because her father was rich, or because of her figure. She was chosen because she was willing to do what was expected and something more.

Men, what would happen if you treated your wives like a queen? What if you sought to learn her expectations and then set out to exceed them all? And wives, what does your husband expect? How could you exceed those expectations? What would it do for your marriage to always go the extra mile? In Matthew 5:41 Jesus said *"Whoever compels you to go one mile, go with them two."* It is interesting to realize that the law at that time said that a Roman soldier had the right to require any male, at any time, to drop what he was doing and carry the soldier's pack for one mile. You can imagine that at the end of the mile most people were quite resentful and quick to put the pack down and go back to what they were doing. Jesus says tell the soldier "I will carry it an extra mile even though I don't have to." That is the mentality of someone in God's Kingdom. Live the life of a servant, not begrudgingly but willingly. We should be like Jonathan's armor bearer who said to him "Do all that is in your heart for I am with you."

There is a store called Nordstrom's that has become famous for service that goes the extra mile. Jeanie and I enjoy shopping there. However there isn't one in Western Michigan where we live. So a few years ago while traveling to a town that did have a Nordstrom's I went shopping. Upon reaching my hotel room I realized I had purchased something in the wrong size. When I called the store the salesman asked "Where are you?" When I told him he brought the right sized item right to my hotel. Have you ever shopped in a department store that would do that? That is going beyond what is expected.

Matthew 5:16 says *"Let your light shine before men, that they may see your good deeds and praise your Father in heaven."* This is what Jesus was talking about. Carrying the soldier's pack twice as far as required would be a bright light in the soldier's face. And when you and I, in our work places and in our relationships, learn what is expected and then exceed it we too will stand out like "a city on a hill." People will say "I want whatever they have got."

CHAPTER 21

WISDOM IS BETTER THAN STRENGTH

"It's better to be wise than strong: intelligence outranks muscle any day. Strategic planning is the key to warfare; to win, you need a lot of good counsel."

Proverbs 24:5-6 (Message)

Solomon again is giving us a God inspired recipe for synergy; for achieving success beyond the average. This time the three ingredients he gives are wisdom, planning, and counsel. Let's take a look at these three ingredients.

Wisdom:

Solomon makes a very similar comment about the superiority of wisdom over strength in Ecclesiastes 9:14-18 but there he takes a little extra time to elaborate. He says, *"There was once a small city with only a few people in it. And a powerful king came against it, surrounded it and built huge siege works against it. Now there lived in that city a man poor but wise and he saved the city by his wisdom. But nobody remembered that poor man. So I said, "Wisdom is better than strength." But the poor man's wisdom is despised, and his words are no longer heeded.*

The quiet words of the wise are more to be heeded than the shouts of a ruler of fools. Wisdom is better than weapons of war, but one sinner destroys much good."

Wisdom is such an important ingredient. That is why Solomon says in Proverbs 4:7 that *"Wisdom is the principle thing."* When a person accepts Jesus, God comes and lives in their heart. Their heart is now filled but unfortunately the same is not automatically true of their head. You can have a full heart and an empty head. That is why scripture says we must "renew our minds." Wisdom comes only to those who are willing to pay the price. No one is born wise.

Here are five scriptural instructions to obtaining wisdom

1. Value wisdom and desire it.

Proverbs 17:16 (Message) says *"Why is there in the hand of a fool the purchase price for wisdom since he has no heart for it?"*

And in Proverbs 1:7 *"The fear of the LORD is the beginning of knowledge, but fools despise wisdom and discipline."*

These verses make it clear that a fool may even have within their reach everything necessary to obtain wisdom but if they do not desire it or if they despise it, wisdom will not come to them. We should desire it like it was a precious jewel, because it is worth more than rubies.

2. To receive wisdom we must ask God for it.

He is the one Who has it and Who can freely give it. Remember Solomon, who is giving us the advice we are studying in this book, received his wisdom by asking God for it.

James 1:5 says, *"If any of you lacks wisdom, let him ask of God, Who gives to all liberally and without reproach, and it will be given to him."*

3. We must receive instruction from God's Word.

James 1:21 says, *"Receive with meekness the implanted word, which is able to save your souls."*

The way to receive God's word is humbly. It may seem silly but we often need to remind ourselves that God is right and that He is way smarter than we are. Whatever God says in His Word is true. If God says something is wrong it is wrong. And the reason it is wrong is because God said it was wrong. It is quite simple, really. As the Creator of the world He is right. He doesn't just know the rules, He wrote the rules.

If you have spent much time around three-five year old children perhaps you have had one of those conversations where they ask a question such as "Can I play in the street?" and you answer "No" to which the child responds "Why?" You then explain that he could be hit by a car. The child thinks about it and says "Why?" You may even answer again, explaining that "cars are fast and heavy and cannot

IF GOD SAYS SOMETHING IS WRONG IT IS WRONG. AND THE REASON IT IS WRONG IS BECAUSE GOD SAID IT WAS WRONG.

stop quickly, even if they want to." The child again asks "Why?" To which you respond with the only answer that will end the questions; "Because I said so." Although you don't mind the child learning, you want to ensure that they accept and act on your advice. You realize that your four year old must accept your instruction. The child needs to accept that you know best even when they can't grasp the reasons. As funny as those exchanges are, God requires the same of us. In fact there are several places in scripture where He gives instructions and then for an explanation He just says "For I am the Lord." In many ways it's sort of like God saying "because I said so," which leads right in to number four.

4. Accept God's Word as His voice and authority in your life.

Proverbs 10:8 states, *"The wise in heart will receive commands, but a prating fool will fall."*

There is a saying that says, "A man with a watch always knows what time it is, but a man with two watches is never quite sure." There should be only one authority in your life, only one compass directing you. If we try to accept God's standard on one issue and invent our own on the next, and on the third we poll the audience, we have become a reed blown in the wind. We are like a man with a room full of clocks who now has no idea what the real time is. Only God has the real time. Only He is the source of truth. That truth by the way is not relative. It doesn't matter how devotedly someone chooses to rely on a broken coo coo clock to give them the time of day. God's truth is still the truth in their life whether they acknowledge it or not.

5. Realize that Jesus is the supreme manifestation of the wisdom of God.

1 Corinthians 1:30 says, *"But of Him you are in Christ Jesus, Who became for us wisdom from God—and righteousness and sanctification and redemption."*

Colossians 2:3, speaking of Jesus says, *"in whom are hidden all the treasures of wisdom and knowledge."*

To receive wisdom we must go beyond accepting Jesus as a nice historical figure. To truly embrace wisdom is to fully embrace Jesus. That means making Him Lord of your life. We must receive His word and chose to live by it.

The second ingredient in this recipe for synergy is planning. Our saying of wisdom for this chapter worded it this way, "Strategic planning is the key to warfare." In other translations it reads "for planning is key for winning," which is saying that failing to plan is pretty much the same as planning to fail.

Habakkuk 2:2 says, *"Write the vision and make it plain on tablets, that he may run who reads it."* This verse may be short but it has a lot to teach about the importance and process of planning.

First, a plan needs a vision. Without a vision you don't know what to plan for. Simply put, a vision is a clear picture of a desired future. Many people believe they have a vision. But they have never written it down nor have they considered what steps are necessary to realize that vision. At that point what they have is more like a daydream. Habakkuk 2:2 shows us

IF A VISION IS FROM GOD IT WILL ALMOST ALWAYS REQUIRE MORE THAN JUST YOU TO BE ACCOMPLISHED.

that a vision should be written down. First, this causes us to fully articulate ourselves. While still in your head a partial vision can easily appear more complete than it is.

Second, it allows others to participate as well. If a vision is from God it will almost always require more than just you to be accomplished. God likes teamwork; a written vision is easy for others to latch on to.

Thirdly, this is where planning steps in. It must be written in a way that those who read it can run. That means the steps are explained. It means that plans are made showing how to realize the vision. It shows how each person can participate.

Sometimes we make the mistake of believing that only businesses should have plans. But what about your marriage? What about your finances? When you search your heart do you see the vision God has planted in there for those areas of your life? Perhaps it isn't very clear because you haven't spent much time clarifying it. Can your spouse run with the vision you have? Does your spouse even know of the vision you have? Wisdom, planning, and counsel. These can be applied anywhere in your life where you want success.

There was a study done of Yale graduates and it was found that 3% of them had already written out their goals. After 20 years those 3% that wrote out their goals had attained those. The other 97% predictably had not. The best indicator of where you will be 10 or 20 years from now is your vision, or your goals. It has been over 30 years since my wife Jeanie and I returned from serving as missionaries in Mexico with a God given vision to pastor a church. I remember having dinner with another local pastor and his wife. They asked "What sort of church are you going to pastor?" I responded "a big church." The pastor's wife said "You mean 500 people?" to which I replied "Oh no, we're going to have thousands and thousands of people." She quickly responded, "I would never want a church that big! I just want to sit in the front row, raise one hand in worship, and hold my coffee in the other. I want to have 50 or 60 people. That is all I need to be happy." It has been over 30 years and you can still find their church. Guess what, she will be sitting on the front row in front of 50-60 people worshiping with a coffee in her hand. Our church now runs several thousand in weekend attendance. We haven't reached the size of church we envisioned yet, but we are well on our way.

A vision by itself doesn't guarantee anything unless you are willing to plan it out and pursue those plans. You have to be willing to put in the effort. Philippians 3:13 says, *"Brethren, I do not count myself to have apprehended; but one thing I do, forgetting those things which are behind and reaching forward to those things which are ahead."* Along the way you're going to have set backs and make mistakes. Not everything will work out according to plan. But that is no excuse not to have one. In the very next verse Habakkuk talks about the waiting. Verse 3 says, *"For the vision is yet for an appointed time; But at the end it will speak, and it will not lie. Though it tarries, wait for it; because it will surely come."*

The third thing Solomon talks to us about is counsel. "To win, you need a lot of good counsel." All counsel is not equal. In the previous chapter we looked at how Solomon's son brought the combined success of his father Solomon and his grandfather David to screeching halt by listening to bad counsel. He caused a revolt and split the kingdom in two by going against the counsel of his father's advisors and instead choosing the advice of his peers.

Andy Stanley in his book The Next Generation Leader wrote, "It is no coincidence that Solomon, the wisest man who ever lived, wrote more about seeking counsel than any other biblical writer. The man who seemed to need it the least was the most convinced of its necessity. The other interesting thing about Solomon's insistence upon seeking counsel is that he was a king. Kings don't need counsel, do they? They are supreme rulers. Throughout the history of Israel, God installed kings who needed counsel. Some sought it, others did not. Those who did not generally paid a high price in their leadership."

How true that is. There are two sure fire recipes for failure. First is to take no one's advice and the second is to take everyone's advice. Since we must be wise about whom we allow to speak into our lives, let's look at some biblical criteria by which we can select counselors.

1. Find counselors who have proven results. This is where Rehoboam made his mistake. Instead of judging the counselors based on their results, he chose to select them based on other criteria. The Bible doesn't tell us much about the advisors who steered him except to say that they were young. Perhaps that is all we are told because that was all the criteria Rehoboam used. He was several thousand years ahead of Woodstock yet he didn't seem to trust anyone over 30.

A few years ago someone came to me very excited about their business plan. They were going to build a certain type of home in some good school districts. They assured me they would make millions and wanted to see if I would invest. I knew that they had never built before. And I knew several extremely experienced builders who were struggling. So I said let me see how things go for the first year before I do any investing. I am truly sad to say I was right to hold off. That man lost everything. No matter what you are learning there is always a learning curve. It takes a while to get good at something. Find counselors who have advanced beyond the learning curve.

This means if you are having marriage trouble don't ask someone who has been divorced four times for counsel. It is obvious whatever they are doing is not working. Especially in relationships it seems the less qualified someone is to give advice the more likely they are to offer it. Find someone who has experience achieving the results you are looking for.

2. Seek loving counsel. It is important that the people you trust for advice are concerned for your success. Hebrews 12:6 says, *"The Lord corrects the people He loves"* (Contemporary English version).

THE LESS QUALIFIED SOMEONE IS TO GIVE ADVICE THE MORE LIKELY THEY ARE TO OFFER IT

God doesn't teach and correct us because He just wants to hear Himself talk. He does it because He loves us. All else being equal a person who genuinely desires for you to succeed will give better advice and give it in a more effective way. Proverbs 27:6 says, *"Faithful are the wounds of a friend."*

3. Ask questions of those who may have answers. Proverbs 20:5 says, *"Counsel in the heart of a wise man is like water in a deep well, but a man of understanding draws it out."* Notice it didn't say that a wise man is like a sprinkler, and everyone who gets near him will get splattered with wisdom. It said he is a well. And not just any well but a deep well. This means getting that wisdom out will require some work on your part. A wise man understands that unsolicited advice is seldom taken. A wise man is not about to *"cast his pearls before swine."* If you want answers then ask questions. Draw the wisdom out of the well. Proverbs 15:12 says, *"A scoffer does not love one who corrects him, nor will he go to the wise."* Prove that you are not a scoffer; ask questions.

I have visited many churches where I immediately noticed things that the pastors could do to improve their service, increase membership, or solve some problem. But if the visit comes and goes without the pastor asking me to share those observations I have learned it is best to keep them to myself. Most times when I try to give advice as an unsolicited act of kindness it backfires. It turns out that they aren't ready to hear it. They still haven't given up hope that doing things their way will work. They don't take the advice and so my advice, in addition to not being helpful, may even offend them or make them uncomfortable.

4. Be open to new thoughts. As simple as this sounds, you might be surprised how many people think they are seeking advice when really all they want is to find someone to tell them they were right all along. If you want advice on how to fix your marriage, are you ready to have someone tell you that you are a part of the problem? That is why people love to listen to motivational speakers. You get all excited about giving a 110% but that speaker doesn't know your situation. He doesn't pass judgment on your strategy. But when you find an experienced person who wants to help you, and you ask them "What should I do?" Be ready to make changes. If you could get where you want to go by doing what you are already doing, most often, you would be there by now. Proverbs 15:14: *"The heart of him who has understanding seeks knowledge."* Be looking for proven, divinely inspired new thoughts.

5. Get a mentor. If you want to get better at playing Ping-Pong what do you need to do? Find someone better than you at Ping-Pong and learn from them. That is true in sports, it is true in business, it is true in finance, and it is true in marriage.

When Jeanie and I first moved to Mexico as missionaries the first church we pastored split, and we were ministerially plateaued for two years. So we went out to an Indian Village where I was mentored by a pastor who had started over 150 churches. His church was the biggest building in town and on special occasions there would be 10,000 people attending. They couldn't fit in the building! That was one of the smartest moves I ever made. I found someone who was good at what I wanted to do, and I learned from him.

The Bible is filled with examples. Ruth had Naomi. Esther had Mordecai. Joshua had Moses. Timothy had Paul. Elisha had Elijah. The disciples had Jesus. In every one of those examples the reason for their success was their mentor.

Getting counsel will often be the difference between success and failure. So many people just ask whoever is nearby. That is ridiculous; it is like attending a church just because it is the closest one to your house. Finding the right person will often be a challenge. In fact, if it is too easy I suggest you double-check your choice.

When we were missionaries in Mexico we would watch as new missionaries came down. Learning a new culture and a new language is very challenging. For some it proved overwhelming. It was amazing to watch how predictably many of these frustrated missionaries would find each other. Instead of getting around a missionary or a native pastor who was really making a difference, who would challenge them to speak more Spanish, to dream big, and to push through the challenges, they were drawn to other missionaries who had settled for doing something less aggressive. Something that didn't require them to improve their language skills or deepen their immersion and understanding of the culture. It seems that being around successful missionaries was intimidating.

AT WHATEVER POINT YOU CHOOSE TO NO LONGER BE STRETCHED BY OTHERS, THAT IS THE BEGINNING OF YOUR DECLINE

They preferred to stick with people who wouldn't make them feel like there was any additional effort needed. I am not picking on missionaries. In fact, I love them. Even the ones in our story deserve a lot of credit for having been willing to get as far as they did, leaving their country, culture, and language behind. The truth is there are examples of that behavior in virtually every arena of life. The lesson is that at whatever point you choose to no longer be stretched by others, that is the beginning of your decline. There is a saying that says "Rivers and men are made crooked by following the path of least resistance." How true it is.

Elisha had the wisdom to leave his father's field and become Elijah's disciple. He had a vision of what he wanted his ministry to be like. He asked Elijah for a double portion of his anointing. He had a plan that he wasn't willing to compromise. On the last day of his life on earth Elijah offered Elisha to stay behind several times but Elisha knew one of the steps in his plan was to be there when Elijah was taken to heaven, and Elisha would not be detoured. He spent 20 years being mentored and listening to Elijah. And when Elisha died he was one miracle short of doubling the number of miracles that his mentor Elijah had performed. It seems Elijah's dream would only almost come true until you look In 2 Kings 13:21 which says, *"Once while some Israelites were burying a man, suddenly they saw a band of raiders; so they threw the man's body into Elisha's tomb. When the body touched Elisha's bones, the man came to life and stood up on his feet."* That clinched it! Elisha doubled the number of recorded miracles as his mentor just as he had envisioned. Never underestimate the power of an endeavor which is chosen wisely, planned carefully and filled with good counsel.

CHAPTER 22

DON'T CAST YOUR PEARLS BEFORE SWINE

"Wise conversation is way above the head of fools. In a serious discussion they haven't a clue."

Proverbs 24:7 (Message)

Jesus restates this same principle in Matthew 7:6. He says it this way, *"Don't give what is holy to dogs, nor cast your pearls before swine. Least they trample them underfoot and turn and tear you in pieces."*

In both of these scriptures we are being given the same warning. The warning is to not take what is holy or special, anything of exceptional value, and share it with just anyone. Have you ever made that mistake? Perhaps you had a special experience, something spiritual you discovered in the Bible. You were very excited but when you shared it, that person could care less. Perhaps it was worse. Perhaps, as Jesus said, they turned on you and mocked you for it.

In Matthew 7:5 Jesus says, *"Hypocrites, first remove the plank out of your own eye, then you will be able to see clearly to remove the speck out of your brother's eye."* The first step to recognizing with whom you can share valuable information is to be aware of your own condition. Are you sensitive to what others are sharing with you? Or do you consider yourself to be the connoisseur of everything spiritual. Paul, who saw Jesus in a vision, who wrote most of the new testament, toured parts of heaven and wrote about it, didn't even consider himself to "have arrived." If Paul still had more to learn, then I know you and I do.

I like what Lester Sumrall said. "If you graduate today and don't learn anything tomorrow you are already behind." We should all strive to be lifelong learners. We must also be careful, however, not to let anyone take the wind out of our sails.

Solomon talks more about this clueless fool in Proverbs 26:4-5. He says, *"Don't answer a fool according to his folly, least you also be like him. Answer a fool according to his folly, least he be wise in his own eyes."*

At first this is confusing. Solomon says do answer a fool and don't answer a fool in the same verse. What is he trying to say? He is saying that with a fool you can't win. A conversation with them is a lose, lose scenario. As we see in Proverbs 24:7, *"serious conversation is over their head."* On one hand you can answer them, making an attempt to convince them of their error. But they won't understand you. If you aren't careful you will lose your composure in a heated debate and your behavior will be as wrong as theirs. But if you choose to avoid engaging in a no win debate the fool will feel certain that they are right. Both approaches end unpleasantly. So which do you chose? Only God knows, but the good news is that if you seek the guidance of the Holy Spirit, He can lead you. Only He knows which is the best road to choose in each individual case.

Solomon wants us not to be surprised when we run into someone who just does not want to learn. These people have already decided they know everything they need to know. Proverbs 26:16 says, *"The lazy man is wiser in his own eyes than seven men who answer sensibly."* That is very contrary to the life of a wise man. To him, being corrected is a valuable experience. Proverbs 6:23 puts it this way, *"For the commandment is a lamp, and the law a light; Reproofs of instruction are the way of life."*

Nobody is saying you should become a junkie for negative feedback. Criticism is never hard to find. It is pretty easy to locate a doubting Thomas who will say, "That will never work. Why bother. Your idea is dumb etc…" Solomon isn't saying that you should love to be insulted. A wise man loves to be corrected because he knows where to look for correction. He doesn't go around throwing his wisdom in front of people who won't value it. He seeks out wise individuals who care enough about his success to tell him when he is out of line, and he values their advice. (Proverbs 27:6) *"Faithful are the wounds of a friend."* He relishes correction from the wise. That is very different than seeking hecklers.

Mark 4:24 says, "Be careful what you hear." A lot of people have the idea that the wiser they are the more worldly influence they are able to withstand. Sort of like movie ratings, PG 13 is supposed to mean that children under 13 may lack the discernment to handle some of the content or thematic elements. Some people assume that with increased wisdom will come increased capacity for exposure to worldliness. Nothing could be further from the truth.

CONSTANT EXPOSURE TO WORLDLINESS DIMINISHES NOT HEIGHTENS YOUR ABILITY TO SEE IT FROM A GODLY PERSPECTIVE

The wiser you are the less you will allow yourself to be exposed to garbage. In the Amplified version Mark 4:24 says, *"He said to them, be careful what you are hearing. The measure [of thought and study] you give [to the truth you hear] will be the measure [of virtue and knowledge] that comes back to you and more [besides] will be given to you who hear."* Wisdom's heightened ability to discern wickedness from godliness comes not from increased exposure to worldliness but from increased exposure to godliness. When, through wisdom, you are guarding your eyes and ears and you accidentally come across a television program filled with crass humor that celebrates sinful behavior, you will see it perhaps for the first time for what it really is, repulsive. Constant exposure to worldliness diminishes not heightens your ability to see it from a godly perspective. But increased exposure to God's Word will bring increased understanding.

God's Word is living and powerful sharper than a two edged sword. When you meditate on it you will not be disappointed. I have studied and preached on passages of scripture and then later listened to another preacher teach on the same passage, and I suddenly felt like a kindergartner. The verse exploded with new meaning. The moment you think you have arrived is the moment it is proven that you haven't. Paul said "I do not consider myself to have arrived." Surely neither have we. Let's not be that fool to whom serious discussions are out of reach. Seek wisdom, and it will be found.

CHAPTER 23

THE IMPORTANCE OF REPUTATION

"He that devises to do evil shall be called a mischievous person"

Proverbs 24:8

An additional verse that reinforces this principle is in Proverbs 22:1. *"A good name is to be chosen rather than great riches, loving favor, rather than silver or gold."* I believe that in today's society if you offered people great riches in exchange for their reputation, you would have a lot of takers. In our society riches are greatly over-valued and reputation under-valued. Ecclesiastes 7:1 says, *"A good name is better than precious ointment in the day of death and in the day of birth."* Solomon is telling us the value of reputation. Integrity is the currency of our life. It will determine who will associate with you and who will not. It will determine with whom you can do business and with whom you cannot. If you think I am exaggerating for emphasis I am not. How many of you realize your credit score will determine who will lend you money and at what rate? The better your score, the more people are going to want to lend you money and the cheaper they are going to want to give it to you. Technically speaking, your credit score is just a mathematical representation of your likeliness to meet your commitments based on your previous behavior. When you told the car dealership and the telephone company you would pay them so much per month did you do it? Or do you frequently disregard your commitments to due dates? There is so much more than a credit score that has to do with your reputation.

EVEN A SEEMINGLY SMALL INCIDENT CAN TOTALLY RUIN A SOLID REPUTATION

Solomon talked about this again in Ecclesiastes 10:1. *"Dead flies putrefy the perfumer's ointment and cause it to give off a foul odor. So is a little folly to one respected for wisdom and honor."* Solomon is pointing out that even a seemingly small incident can totally ruin a solid reputation. I read a fantastic example of this. Woody Hayes was a very well respected coach for Ohio State. He was one of the most notable leaders in the history of college football. But when his name is mentioned many people think "Isn't that the guy who hit a kid?" During an extremely intense and important game, a player from the other team was running down the sideline toward a long and certain touchdown. Woody Hayes the coach, unable to control himself, stepped off the sideline onto the field and struck down the player himself. It was an unthinkable act that occurred at the end of a long and distinguished career. Yet that one act became his legacy.

Bad reputations are very sticky and hard to shake. God talks about David and calls him a man after his own heart. But three thousand years later if you say "David" people think "Bathsheba." When you say "Sampson" the next name on people's mind is "Delilah." A bad reputation is very hard to kill.

Oral Roberts said, "Not having integrity is like not having a name or country. Without integrity I could never have accomplished the things that God called me to do." I believe that is true. Without integrity you and I will not be able to fulfill the calling on our lives. One thing that every Christian should be known for is their integrity.

The very definition of integrity is to be whole or morally complete. Perhaps you have heard the story about a couple who went through the Kentucky Fried Chicken drive-thru. The attendant handed the man his bag of food and the man drove off. Instead of getting the food he had ordered, when he opened the bag there was over $5,000 dollars in cash plus a lot of checks. The store manager had placed the deposit into one of the bags and it was given to him by mistake. The man quickly returned to the store to hand it back. The manager was so thankful he told the man, "Please stay right here while I call the newspaper. They should do an article about you and take your picture. Not just anyone would return that much cash." The man said "Please don't do that. I don't want my picture taken; you see the woman with me in the car is not my wife." That man does not have true integrity. He is not morally complete. He may have done right in one area but he was doing wrong in another.

Here is another story that I feel powerfully illustrates the importance of integrity. The story is true. It is told by Pat Williams. He calls it the Paradox of Powerfully.

> Mr. Hoess was a loving husband and father, and a devout Catholic. His five children respected and adored him. He was also a business leader. He had grown prosperous as a farmer, largely because of his administrative skills.
>
> One of Mr. Hoess's acquaintances in the government took note of how he managed his farming business. He was offered a post in the government, where he proved himself very capable. This led to a series of promotions, and Mr. Hoess rose rapidly in a series of government offices.
>
> Mr. Hoess had a regular routine every day: breakfast with his wife and children, then off to work—sometimes

pausing to enjoy the fragrance of the flowers in his well-tended garden. Mr. Hoess worked diligently at his job, conducting staff meetings, making important decisions, reading reports, issuing orders. At the end of the day, he arrived home, where his children happily greeted him at the front door. They looked forward to his arrival because he often brought them little gifts.

His loyalty and patriotism earned him the trust of the most important man in the national government. That man, whose name was Adolf Hitler, rewarded Rudolf Hoess by making him Kommandant of the Auschwitz extermination complex in southern Poland. Mr. Hoess's mission: To increase the killing efficiency of the camp to a level of ten thousand dead every twenty four hours. Mr. Hoess was very good at his job, and he had no trouble meeting his quota.

From the bedroom window of his comfortable brick-walled house in the country, Mr. Hoess could see the chimneys of the camp. The smoke from those chimneys darkened the skies as thousands of human bodies were cremated, day after day, night after night, twenty-four/seven. He was proud of his work. Under his efficient management, Auschwitz exterminated 2.5 million people.

Rudolf Hoess was raised to work hard and live a productive life. He was a loving family man, a devout Catholic, and possibly the greatest mass murderer in human history. Why didn't he see any contradiction in these various roles he played? Because Rudolf Hoess had compartmentalized his soul. He had constructed a wall of separation between his home life and his vocational life, between his Sunday morning faith and his job during the week as the Kommandant of Hell.

Ninety five percent of his life may have been exemplary but that doesn't matter. The devil doesn't need you to give him every area of your life, just one is enough. That is why integrity has to do with the whole person. Some people mistakenly believe that integrity is about believing the right things. But Peter, on the day of Pentecost as he preached the opening sermon of the church said, "Be saved from this perverse generation." Christianity isn't just what you believe. It is what you do with what you believe.

THE DEVIL DOESN'T NEED YOU TO GIVE HIM EVERY AREA OF YOUR LIFE, JUST ONE IS ENOUGH.

What Solomon is telling us is that a good name is more important than money, and that a good name needs to be pursued daily. It takes years of hard work to build it, but it can be destroyed very quickly. So let's take a moment to explore four things that can help us to guard our integrity.

1. Accountability. Proverbs 18:1 says *"A man who isolates himself seeks his own desire; He rages against all wise judgment."* When a person isolates themselves they no longer have anyone who can say to them, "What's going on in your life?" They become even less likely to have someone who can say to them, "This thing that you are doing or saying is not right." When there is no one who can speak into your life you are in trouble. All of us need someone whom we respect in the Lord to speak into our life.

2. Righteous Fellowship. 1 Corinthians 15:33 states, *"Don't be deceived; evil company corrupts good habits or good morals."* We have dedicated a whole chapter to this concept so I don't need to revisit the topic too deeply here. Except to emphasize that your friendships will deeply impact your decisions and your behavior. We are called to be salt and light. Scripture doesn't forbid contact with the ungodly. It does teach you to be discerning and careful about the influences you welcome into your life. As we have seen here one wrong move can cost your integrity and tarnish your reputation beyond repair.

3. Honesty. Jesus said in John 8:32, *"The truth will set you free."* The flip side of that truth is that dishonesty will keep us in bondage. We need to be honest with ourselves and we need to be honest with others. James 5:16 says, *"Confess your sins one to another, pray for one another, that you may be healed."* Our culture today is confused. They are confused by their own ever changing standards of right and wrong which are trying to keep up with political correctness. Even the very meaning of honesty is under attack as evidenced by a president who famously stated in stark contrast to the evidence, "I did not tell a lie." The only reliable standard is God's Word. Be honest with yourself. Don't accept any culturally altered definitions of truth that allow for semantics and misdirection. Walk in the freedom that only comes from honesty.

4. Humility. Pride thinks it is capable of success apart from humble obedience to God and adherence to the standards of the Word. It won't admit weakness or seek counsel. Say this with me, "I could fall." We all need to admit that to ourselves and realize that the enemy is prowling around, seeking an arrogant, careless soul to devour. Only through humility can you escape him. James 4:6-7 declares, *"But He gives more grace. Therefore He says: 'God resists the proud, but gives grace to the humble.' Therefore submit to God. Resist the devil and he will flee from you."* Humility submits itself to God and recognizes its need for God.

There is a story that illustrates the value of integrity and the scarcity of it that I have read in so many different places I feel certain it must be historically accurate.

Sir Arthur Conan Doyle decided to play a practical joke on 12 well respected men that he knew. He sent each a telegram with the same message, "Flee at once, all is discovered." Within 24 hours all but two of them had left the country. Obviously there was a lack of integrity among them. That is not the kind of legacy that we want to leave.

Home is where integrity matters most. In the Message translation, Psalm 101:1-8 says, *"My theme song is God's love and justice, and I'm singing it right to You, God. I'm finding my way down the road of right living, but how long before You show up? I'm doing the very best I can, and I'm doing it at home, where it counts. I refuse to take a second look at corrupting people and degrading things. I reject made-in-Canaan gods and stay clear of contamination. The crooked in heart keep their distance; I refuse to shake hands with those who plan evil. I put a gag on the gossip who bad-mouths his neighbor; I can't stand arrogance. But I have my eye on salt-of-the-earth people— they're the ones I want working with me; Men and women on the straight and narrow—these are the ones I want at my side. But no one who traffics in lies gets a job with me; I have no patience with liars. I've rounded up all the wicked like cattle and herded them right out of the country. I purge God's city of all who make a business of evil."*

Where there is no integrity there is no trust and where there is no trust there is no authority. It is there among those who know you best that you will see the effects the soonest. Where there is no trust, relationships dissolve because trust is the foundation of relationships, and trust is easily destroyed.

As we close this chapter I want to emphasize one thing. Trust can be rebuilt. Perhaps you know your name is already tarnished; the damage may be visible with your loved ones. To rebuild trust you must confess your sin and repent. That means saying, "I am sorry. I was wrong," and then being willing to make yourself accountable to walk out that repentance.

What really brings satisfaction in life are relationships and they are built on integrity. I have been in some very nice homes and I have been in mud huts, with thatched roofs, no electricity, no running water, and no bathrooms. It is not stuff that makes your life great;

it is relationships. Many multimillionaires are miserable and there are people who could not tell you where their next meal is coming from who have peace and have great relationships. But you can't have those things without integrity.

CHAPTER 24

ADVERSITY COMES TO US ALL

"If you faint in the day of adversity your strength is small"

Proverbs 24:10

If your idea of success is the absence of adversity your definition is not biblical. In Matthew chapter 7 Jesus tells the parable of the man who built his house upon the rock. Did you ever notice that the same storms, wind, and floods came against the righteous man's house as destroyed the foolish man's home? His righteousness didn't save him from the storm; it saw him through it. Job 5:7 says, *"Yet man is born to trouble, like the sparks fly upward."* That verse is probably not underlined in your Bible, written on any plaques on your walls, or on the bumper of your car, but it is still true. You are going to have obstacles;

IF YOUR IDEA OF SUCCESS IS THE ABSENCE OF ADVERSITY YOUR DEFINITION IS NOT BIBLICAL.

there will be circumstances that come against you. As sure as you try to move forward there will be opposition.

1 Peter 4:12 says, *"Beloved, do not think it strange concerning the fiery trial which is to try you, as though some strange thing happened to you."* That is another one of those verses that you rarely see stuck to the refrigerator. Based on their reactions it seems many Christians don't realize these scriptures exist. When they are faced with difficulty they respond by saying "What is happening? I mean, I pray, I read my Bible, I love God." They seem to believe that unless they are doing something wrong they should be exempt from all forms of difficulty. If doing good would result in nothing but a cushy life of ease then what it is Galatians 6:9 doing in our Bibles? It says, *"Let us not grow weary in doing good, for in due season we shall reap if we faint not."* The terms "growing weary" and "fainting" don't sound like the results of a life of ease. Jesus never promised us a cake walk. But notice that in due season the rewards of doing good will come. Doing good does bring blessing. Solomon is just warning us that in between the blessings and the reward, while we wait for the due season to come, there will be difficulty.

The Bible is meant to be an encouragement to us to overcome the feelings of frustration; the temptation to just throw in the towel. We are not the only ones who have ever felt those things. Think about David, Moses, Joshua, and Jeremiah. They all faced discouragement. In fact, Jeremiah said at one point, "God, I just want to get a hotel in Arizona and get away from it all." Well he nearly said that. What he actually said was, "I just want a place for wayfaring travelers in the desert." That sounds a lot like a hotel in Arizona to me. He just wanted to get away. God has something to say to us when we feel that way. He said it to Joshua in Joshua chapter 1 and verse 7, *"Only be strong and courageous"* then again God said in verse 9, *"Have I not commanded you to be strong and of good courage"* and again in verse 18, *"Only be strong and of good courage."* Obviously Joshua must have been feeling something less than wonderful and facing something that wasn't easy or else God wouldn't have told him so many times to be strong. Joshua was feeling discouraged. This is the guy who lead Israel miraculously across the Jordan River and had the walls of Jericho knocked down by God Himself. Yet he was discouraged. This should be an encouragement to us. Faith doesn't mean you are never tempted to be discouraged, never tempted to be afraid, never tempted to give up. It just means that you keep going. Perhaps you feel weak, but the Bible says, "Let the weak say 'I am strong!'"

If adversity will come to us all, how do we handle it? Do we sit back and say, "Well I guess all this bad stuff is supposed to happen, so I might as well try and wait it out." No, that is not what I see the men of faith doing in the Bible. They rose up, took courage in God, and by faith pressed on. Are you ready to do the same? Did you know that you are equipped to do the same? Paul says in 2 Corinthians 4:13, *And since we have the same spirit of faith, according to what is written, "I believed and therefore I spoke," we also believe and therefore speak."* That is a very important truth. Scripture says that you have the same spirit of faith as King David, as the apostle Paul. It worked the same for the heroes of the Bible as it can for you and for me.

What is the spirit of faith? Paul says there are two parts. "I believed and therefore I spoke." There is a believing part and a speaking part and it functions the same every time. The most precious possession that you could possibly have on this earth is the spirit of faith. David had the spirit of faith when he was only about 17 years old. Joshua and Caleb had it when they were 85. It has nothing to do with how old you are. It has nothing to do with your gender or ethnicity. The spirit of faith has to do with your connection with God.

Smith Wigglesworth was a man who knew a thing or two about faith. He said, "If you want the power of God in your life, never look back." Have you ever made a mistake? If you let him, Satan will make a full feature length film of that mistake and play it for you every chance he gets. The devil always wants to draw your attention to the past. If he tries it, I suggest you just reminded him of his future. God, on the other hand, doesn't speak to you about your past. He speaks to you about your future from the perspective of your destiny.

One great example is Gideon found in Judges chapter 6. Gideon was threshing wheat in a wine press. You need to understand that to thresh wheat you need wind, and a wine press is not very breezy. In fact it is a giant bowl with walls for holding grapes. But Gideon was so afraid of being seen by the Midianites that he was hiding in there and trying to thresh the wheat anyway. An angel of the Lord shows up and says "Hail, God is with you mighty man of valor." I am sure he looked around to see who the angel must be talking to; surely it wasn't him. Then Gideon responds like many Christians do, "Well, if God is with us why is there trouble? Shouldn't everything be rosy if God is with us? But, we are being oppressed by the Midianites." The angel responds, "Yes, God knows about the Midianites and that is why I am here. I have come to tell you that God wants you to deliver Israel from them." Now Gideon begins to list the reasons why he couldn't possibly be qualified for the job. "Oh angel, you must be mistaken. I am from the least significant tribe of Israel. We are the Barney Fife tribe, and I am Barney Fife. I am the least significant of the insignificants. My tribe is the smallest tribe, my father's house is the smallest house, and I am the least of his house." Gideon figures God can use others but surely not him. Gideon sees himself as a product of his circumstances and a result of his past shortcomings. Did you notice though that even while Gideon was hiding from the enemy soldiers the angel greeted him, based not on what he had already done, but the greeting was based on what God desired to do through Gideon. The angel called Gideon a "mighty man of valor." You and I would say that eventually that is what he became. God says that is what he always was; he just didn't know it yet. God took two chapters of the Bible to change the way Gideon saw himself.

If you want to change those difficult circumstances that are in your life it will start with changing the way you think. I heard about a fellow who had the family over for a big Sunday lunch and then he fell asleep on the couch. The kids got to him while he was sleeping and they put Limburger cheese on his mustache. Within a few moments he gets a whiff of that smelly cheese and wakes right up. "This room stinks," he says and goes into the TV room where everyone is watching a football game. There he says "this room stinks too." When he gets in the kitchen of course it is stinky in there as well. So he decides to go outside onto the deck. He takes a deep breathe full of Limburger cheese and declares, "The whole world stinks!" When you have the spirit of faith the whole world smells like victory. Wherever you go you don't see defeat, you don't see discouragement. Wherever you are you look around and say, "Oh look! There is some victory over there. I smell some victory over here."

Let's take a look at the very first Passover, the night that proceeded the day that the Israelites were given freedom from Egypt. You could say it was to be the night they would receive their victory. The story is in Exodus chapter 12. God has sent Moses to speak to Pharaoh on behalf of the Israelites and to request that they be released. Nine times God sends various plagues to convince Pharaoh to let them go and nine times Pharaoh acts as if he will release them but changes his mind after the plague is called off. The Israelites know that this 10th plague is different because Moses tells them to prepare in advance. He says, *Take a lamb into your home on the 10th day of the month and keep it until the 14th day. At twilight take the lamb out of your home and kill the lamb."* The Bible tells us in Corinthians, that "Christ, our Passover lamb, has been sacrificed for us." The innocent lamb that they killed was a type of Jesus. It represented the innocent dying for the guilty.

That night the angel of death would pass through Egypt and there would be a tremendous catastrophe. The first born son of every household would die. The children of the Israelites were to be spared. The lamb had died in their place. I want you to ask yourself a question. Did the Israelites have to do anything to receive the benefit of the lamb's sacrifice? Or was everything already done for them? The answer is yes, there was something they needed to do. Moses instructed them to take the blood of the lamb and catch it in a basin.

Then they were to go to door posts of their home and smear the blood with a hyssop branch first on the side then dip the branch again and then on the top of the door. God said, "Wherever I see the blood, I will not allow the destroying angel to enter in." The lamb was dead. The lamb had done its part but the people, all be it a very small thing, did have something to do. They had to apply the blood. This same thing is true today. Revelation 12:11 says, *"And they* (that is you) *overcome him* (that is the devil) *by the blood of the lamb and the word of their testimony."* How do I apply the blood to my situation? I apply it with the word of my testimony. You need to take your hyssop, which would be your tongue, and apply the blood of Jesus by the word of your testimony. The victory you seek has been won for you but you must apply the blood.

Mark 11:23-4 says, *"Whoever says to this mountain, 'Be removed and be cast into the sea,' and does not doubt in his heart, but believes that those things he says will be done, he will have whatever he says."* When you ask most Christians, "What is faith?" they most often answer "Faith is trust, faith is confidence, faith is assurance." I will grant that each of those is true, and a correct answer. However, if you ask Jesus about faith, He answers the question differently. When Jesus talks about faith He doesn't just talk about belief. He said to his disciples, "Whoever will say." Jesus said that faith works for "whosoever will say… and not doubt"

What you say is connected to what you will receive. Yes adversity comes to us all. But if you are walking around saying things like "I just know I am going to be laid off" or "Nothing good ever happens to me" then don't be surprised when your words come to pass. Words are powerful, they always have been.

DON'T BE SURPRISED WHEN YOUR WORDS COME TO PASS

How was the world made? In Genesis 1:1 Scripture says, "In the beginning God created the heavens and the earth and the earth was void." That word "void" means catastrophic, a total mess. Did God look at that void and say "What a mess. Look how dark and ugly it is. No one in the right mind would want anything to do with that place?" If God talked like many Christians today that is about what He would have said. But God didn't talk about what He saw, He talked about what He wanted. If we will talk only about what we see then that is all we are going to get.

Words are powerful enough to affect your situation. Jesus said Matthew 4:4, *"Man shall not live by bread alone, but by every word that precedes out of the mouth of God."* In Isaiah God said *"My word that proceeds out of my mouth shall not return unto me void."* God's Word is powerful. You and I have a copy of His Word. In fact most of us have several copies, the Bible. He didn't give us His Word so we could just bind it in leather and monogram our initials on it. Joshua 1:8 says, *"This book of the law should not depart out of your mouth"* God's Word belongs in your mouth, not on the book shelf. Look at Isaiah 59:21. It says, *"My word which I put in your mouth shall not depart from your mouth, nor from the mouth of your descendants, nor from the mouth of your descendant's descendants says the Lord from this time forth and forevermore."* We are to have God's Word in our mouth.

When Jesus was in the desert and Satan came to tempt him, Jesus began His response the same way every time. "It is written." He said that because God's Word was also in His mouth. The way He faced the enemy is the way that you and I should also face the difficult situations that are sure to come our way. By speaking God's Word.

When David faced the giant, Goliath, who had been insulting the Israelites and God on a daily basis, David spoke to the giant. The giant spoke, then David spoke again, and David ran. David prevailed, cut the giant's head off, and the giant never said anything else again. Whatever the giant is in your life, it should never get the last word.

Matthew 21:21 says *"So Jesus answered and said to them, 'Assuredly, I say to you, if you have faith and do not doubt, you will not only do what was done to the fig tree, but also if you say to this mountain, 'Be removed and be cast into the sea,' it will be done."* Many Christians have the idea that when they are facing a mountain in their life it must be God's will. They will say things like, "God sent me this mountain to teach me a lesson." They will claim that every bad thing that happens to them is somehow God's sovereign will. That is not true. The problem is that it is easy to take the concept of God's sovereignty and apply it in ways the Bible does not. In fact that is contrary to scripture. The Bible does not say that everything that happens is God's will for your life.

1 Timothy 2:4 says that God *"desires all men to be saved and to come to the knowledge of the truth."* Scripture tells us, and I am sure you would agree, that there are many people who die in sin without being saved. Jesus didn't say to the disciples, "if God wills it this mountain will be lifted up and cast into the sea." He said, *"If you had faith."* Notice something will happen only "if you." The idea that absolutely everything that happens is God's will is just not biblical. Jesus wouldn't have told us to pray, "Your will be done on earth as it is in heaven" if God's will was already being done on earth as it is in heaven. If it was God's will for you to have that mountain in your life Jesus would not have taught us how to move it.

A lot of people like the idea of hyper-sovereignty because they feel that our eternal destinies and our lives are too great of a responsibility for God to have left in our hands. They are only half right. It is a great responsibility. In the very beginning with Adam and Eve God chose to give man a free will. That hasn't changed. It is clear in scripture that God gave Adam and Eve a choice, and He gives you and I choices. Our response when faced with choices of what to do and what to say will impact our lives.

Solomon didn't say that if we were strong we would avoid all adversity. He said when the day of adversity comes the strong will not faint. How will they not faint? I believe the key to not fainting in adversity is your faith in God, and according to Jesus the key to your faith is in your words.

CHAPTER 25

RESCUE THE PERISHING (ABORTION)

"Rescue the perishing, don't hesitate to step in and help. If you say, "Hey, that's none of my business," will that get you off the hook? Someone is watching you closely, you know—someone not impressed with weak excuses."
Proverbs 24:11-12 (MSG)

It is Biblical and right for us to help the poor, the downtrodden, the abused. Who are the perishing? I believe that in American society today this applies most directly to the unborn. Abortion in America today is literally an epidemic. In our hospitals and clinics today there is abortion, infanticide, and now much talk about euthanasia. From the decision of Roe versus Wade to 2017 America performed 59,115,995 abortions! That is 53 times more deaths than in all of our wars combined.

I want to clarify right away that it is not my intention to condemn anyone. This message is to renew our minds, to give us a biblical perspective. In the first few centuries, church history reveals that the early church was extremely counter-cultural. The church stood against the unbiblical yet common practices of its day including suicide, euthanasia, and infanticide. The need for the church to be counter-cultural has not expired. In fact as our society becomes increasingly post-Christian the need is ever growing.

To give you a picture of where society is, Princeton University began in 1746 by the Presbyterians to train men for the ministry. Its main purpose was to train pastors. Jonathan Edwards, the preacher who was in great part responsible for the first great awakening in America, was the third president of the University. That was then. Today Peter Singer teaches bioethics at Princeton University. He said on September 11 that he "would kill a baby if it was in the best interest of the baby or of the family as a whole." He wasn't talking about abortion, he was talking about killing a young child. He defends his position with this statement, "Newborn human babies have no sense of their own existence over time, and so killing a newborn baby is never equivalent to killing a person." Peter Singer also said "The notion that human life is sacred just because it's human is medieval." He is a professor at a school that was founded to train pastors. He is recognized as a leading authority, if not the leading authority, on bioethics in America today.

Now let's look at God's perspective. Genesis 9:5 says, *"Surely for your life blood I will demand a reckoning and from the hand of every piece I will require it from the hand of man. From the hand of every man's brother I will require the life of blood the life of man."* God says that the purpose of government is to protect life. That human life is special because He made man in His own image. He breathed into man the breath of life. Man became a living soul. Every person on the face of the earth is immortal. This means that although you have a beginning you will never have an ending. You are going to live someplace for all of eternity.

Today, medical science can detect life inside the womb on the 12th day. That is pretty good but we have to realize God is smarter than scientists. God finds it on the first day. In Psalms 139 the Bible says, *"You shaped me first inside then out. You formed in my mother's womb. I thank you, High God. You're breathtaking. Body and soul, I am marvelously made. I worship in adoration—what a creation! You know me inside and out, You know every bone in my body; You know exactly how I was made, bit by bit, how I how I was sculpted from nothing into something. Like an open book, You watched me grow from conception to birth; all the stages of my life were spread out before You. The days of my life all prepared before I'd even lived one day"* (Message). You and I are not accidents. God knows us. Jeremiah 1:5 says, *"Before I formed you in the womb, I knew you. Before you were born I sanctified you. I ordained you a prophet to the nations."*

God said this about John the Baptist in Luke 1:15. He sent his angel and said, *"He will be great in the sight of the Lord. And shall drink neither wine nor strong drink. He will also be filled with the Holy Spirit, even from his mother's womb."* Then a few verses later Elizabeth was about six months into the pregnancy and Mary, who is pregnant with Jesus, arrives to meet her. Elizabeth says to Mary in Luke 1:44 *"For indeed, as soon as the voice of your greeting sounded in my ears, the babe leaped in my womb for joy."* So three months before birth John the Baptist was having spiritual experiences in the womb! He was communicating with God, aware of the arrival of Jesus.

In 1857 there was a rather famous case that went before the Supreme Court called the Dred Scott case. Perhaps you have heard of it. In this case the Supreme Court made a ruling that African Americans were not protected under the Constitution of the United States. That was a very bad decision. That same court in 1973 made a decision that an unborn child is not protected by the Constitution of the United States. Is the unborn child a person? Are they alive? Do they have emotions? Those were never the questions. The only question was, were they protected in the Constitution of the United States. We as Christians, if we believe the Bible, which all of us should, will recognize that unborn babies are people who God knows, who have spiritual experiences, and for whom God has plans.

We can also see that our Supreme Court has made some very bad decisions. One of those horrible decisions is not to protect the unborn children. At an abortion clinic an abortion will take between 5-10 minutes. If you want to adopt a child that will usually take between 2 and 10 years. The issue is not that the children are unwanted. The argument that these children would be born into families unable to provide financially for all of their needs and are therefore better off not living is, of course, very unbiblical as well as ridiculous. Jesus said "Your life does not consist in the abundance of the things that you possess."

The United Nations says that absolute poverty is living on less than 1 dollar a day. Anything above that is relative poverty. If you try to tell someone who is living on less than 1 dollar a day that their life is not worth living, it is a lie. I have spoken to people in that situation and they would tell you that they still appreciate being alive, and desire to remain alive.

There is a philosophy called "presentism." This simply means that newest is best. Although it may be true that the newest cell phone is superior to the old ones, and the newest computer is faster than the old ones, every idea that comes along is not always better than the previous one. It is obvious that Americans are not doing marriage better today than we used to. The new acceptance of abortion is not a step forward for society, or for women no matter what you have heard. Somewhere near half of the millions of babies killed were women. How are they better off?

What is happening in America is a holocaust. I don't believe it is different than when Adolf Hitler set aside certain people, the Jews, gypsies, and a few other groups and declared they are not human like everyone else. He killed 12,000,000 people over 6,000,000 of them Jews. Joseph Stalin killed 29,000,000 people not that long ago. Pol Pot and the killing fields of Cambodia were 1.7 million. Chairman Mao killed 60,000,000. The unborn babies killed just in the USA will very soon surpass the numbers killed by the worst mass murderer of all time.

How could all this happen? John 3:19 says, *"And this is the condemnation that the light is coming to the world, but men loved darkness rather than light, because their deeds were evil."* Ravi Zacharias who is possibly the foremost Christian philosopher today—says this. "Our ways today are only better than 60 years ago on the surface level. At the core, we are in the same mess as with Hitler and with Chairman Mao. Things have not changed."

I recently read an article where a minister said "I don't vote and I don't think that churches should encourage people to have any sort of moral stance that they take to the voting booth." I was shocked. I will tell you this about myself. I do vote and I believe as Christians we should all vote. We need to take a stand and that is one place in our country where we can take a stand.

Some person will say, "I just don't think you can legislate morality. You can't be prejudiced against somebody else's ideas." Please allow me to point something out. All laws are prejudiced. By its very definition a law is pre-judging, or pre-determining something to be "wrong." Whenever a new law is made it is made so that the next time that act is committed a judgment at that time is not necessary. The law will have previously judged that act to be wrong. If you like to speed, the law is prejudiced against you and you will get tickets. The morality, the opinion,

> **AS CHRISTIANS IF WE ATTEMPT TO NOT LEGISLATE MORALITY, WE JUST ALLOW SOMEONE ELSE'S MORALITY TO BE LEGISLATED.**

and the judgment of someone is going to be legislated. As Christians, if we attempt to not legislate morality, we just allow someone else's morality to be legislated.

Solomon said "Rescue the perishing." Voting and being politically active when there are lives on the line is one way you can do that.

Another thing you can do is pray. Please Mr. or Mrs. Reader, I implore you, stand for what the Bible declares is righteous. 140 years ago the issue at hand in our nation was slavery and the church stood up against it. Today we need to stand up against abortion. Deuteronomy 27:25 says, "Cursed is the one who takes a bribe to slay an innocent person." If we choose to support a candidate who will support the murder of the unborn because we think their fiscal policies will benefit our pocket book, how is that different? When we vote we are hiring or firing politicians. Anyone who goes out and hires a hit man to kill before the law is guilty of murder before the law as well. I believe there is a guilt associated with voting knowingly in support of candidates with murderous agendas. One of our prayers should be that God would forgive us as a nation for our indifference to those perishing.

The second part of what Solomon is telling us was that claiming it wasn't your business won't get you off the hook. God is watching us and He sees through weak excuses. In Revelation 22:12 Jesus said, *"Behold, I am coming quickly. My reward is with Me to give to every man according to his word."* The day will come when God will ask you, "What did you do with what I gave you? How did you treat your spouse? How did you treat your kids? And, what did you do for the perishing?" In Revelation 3:11 Jesus said *"Behold, I'm coming quickly. Hold fast what you have. Let no one take your crown."* As a believer I know that people will be qualified to receive rewards because of things that they did in their life. They can even get rewards for things they didn't do. Perhaps as you read this you are crying out, there is guilt, there are regrets, there is pain, and sorrow. Maybe you say "I participated, I helped somebody have an abortion." Or, "I had an abortion." I want to say something to you. That is why Jesus died. 1 John 1:1 says, *"If we say we have no sin, we deceive ourselves and the truth is not in us."* The Bible says that God has laid upon Him the iniquities of us all. John continues and says, *"If we confess our sin, He is faithful and just to forgive us of our sins and to cleanse us from all unrighteousness."* If you ask forgiveness, as surely as there is a God, He will forgive you.

The late Dr. Summerall told a story about an elderly woman who came to see him. When he asked her what she wanted to see him for, she replied that she had committed adultery. He replied "Well Grandma, tell me about it" and she responded with "When I was in college I had an affair with one of my professors." Dr. Summerall asked, "How long ago was this?" She said "well, this was 51 or 52 years ago." He said "Ma'am, you are a Christian now, and you have asked for forgiveness." She said, "Yes, but it has bothered me every single day of my life." It is so unfortunate that it took this woman 52 years to discover that God truly and fully forgave her the first time she repented and asked forgiveness. Romans 8:1 says, *"Therefore, there is now no condemnation for those who are in Christ Jesus."* Your sins are forgiven. The Bible says God "casts it into the sea of forgetfulness." Corey Tenboom liked to say "And then He puts up a no fishing sign." If there is anything in your past you aren't proud of as it relates to this issue, or any other for that matter, I want to encourage you that if you have asked God for forgiveness it is already yours. You can let it go. God has.

CHAPTER 26

YOUR HOPE WILL NOT BE CUT OFF

"My son, eat honey because it's good and the honeycomb which is sweet to your taste, so shall knowledge and wisdom be to your soul if you have found it. There is a prospect and your hope will not be cut off."

Proverbs 24:13-14

Maybe you started this book thinking, well I guess I should learn what Solomon has to tell me. It will probably be good for me. Perhaps your attitude was sort of like a kid who decides to eat the dreaded vegetables because he regretfully realizes it will pay off. But, by now, you are probably enjoying it. Wisdom has that effect. Solomon is saying here that once your soul gets wisdom it will love it. Your soul will want it. It will be like honey or today we would say candy. Solomon adds that the sweet cherry on the top of what wisdom will bring you is, "the hope that will not be cut off." He used this term once before during these thirty sayings. One chapter earlier in Proverbs, Solomon also talked of being eternally minded (Proverbs 23:18). Solomon reminds us that wisdom brings sweet reward to your soul and life, and none is sweeter than eternal life. Solomon realized that true wisdom is only discovered in finding God. That is not to say that we are saved by wisdom, for it is by grace through faith. Solomon just realizes to know wisdom is to know God and that no wise man would refuse eternal life.

I want to expound some on that "hope" that Solomon refers to. I want to look into what scripture says about eternal life. Satan would love nothing better than to confuse us concerning what the Bible says about eternity. That hope Solomon speaks of Satan desires to steal. Titus 2:13 says *"Looking for the blessed hope and glorious appearing of our great God and Savior Jesus Christ."* Every New Testament author refers to the return of Jesus. Even the short little book of Jude in its one chapter mentions it. Many places in scripture refer to the return of Jesus as the blessed hope.

Jesus said "I go to prepare a place for you." Heaven isn't an idea, it is a real place. Eternity is not uncomplicated. There are only two addresses. Fellowship with God in heaven, or separation from God in what scripture calls the lake of fire, also called the second death in hell. Jesus spoke about hell 33 times. In fact over 90% of what we know from scripture about hell, we know from what Jesus said. Hell is referred to in scripture no less than 167 times. I say that to emphasize that hell is not some hoax that was put together by the church to manipulate people. Hell is found all through the Bible. In fact, in the fundamental doctrines listed in Hebrews chapter 6 it is mentioned as eternal judgment.

We cannot say, "I never heard what it was like because no one who knows about it has ever been back to earth to tell us." Jesus gave us a very vivid picture. In Luke 16:19 Jesus said, *"There was a certain rich man, clothed in purple and fine linen, who fared sumptuously every day."* Please notice how Jesus began this account. He said "There was a certain rich man." Jesus doesn't lie. He doesn't pass things off as truths that aren't real. He said the rich man was "a certain rich man" and he told us that the beggar's name was Lazarus. This was not a parable. This was an account of two men who actually lived and an interaction after their deaths that really took place. When Jesus told parables He didn't use names. As He began parables He would say, "It is like a man who sowed some seed…" (Mark 4:26) and, *"It is like a man who built a house on the ground without a foundation…"* (Luke 6:49). He never referred to any parable as a "certain man." Everything Jesus said about what happened to that rich man and Lazarus is an accurate portrayal of life after death, at a time before Jesus had died and risen again taking captivity captive. It was not just symbolism or illustration.

Here is what Jesus said:

> Luke 17:19-31, *"There was a rich man who was dressed in purple and fine linen and lived in luxury every day. At his gate was laid a beggar named Lazarus, covered with sores and longing to eat what fell from the rich man's table. Even the dogs came and licked his sores. The time came when the beggar died and the angels carried him to Abraham's side. The rich man also died and was buried. In hell, where he was in torment, he looked up and saw Abraham far away, with Lazarus by his side. So he called to him, 'Father Abraham, have pity on me and send Lazarus to dip the tip of his finger in water and cool my tongue, because I am in agony in this fire.'* "*But Abraham replied, 'Son, remember that in your lifetime you received your good things, while Lazarus received bad things, but now he is comforted here and you are in agony. And besides all this, between us and you a great chasm has been fixed, so that those who want to go from here to you cannot, nor can anyone cross over from there to us.' He answered, 'Then I beg you, Father, send Lazarus to my father's house, for I have five brothers. Let him warn them, so that they will not also come to this place of torment.' Abraham replied, 'They have Moses and the Prophets; let them listen to them.' 'No, Father Abraham,' he said, 'but if someone from the dead goes to them, they will repent.' He said to him, 'If*

*they do not listen to Moses and the Prophets, they will not
be convinced even if someone rises from the dead.' "*

Hell is portrayed as a place that is eternal, unquenchable, everlasting fire. The rich man had the greatest surprise of his existence to
find himself in hell. He did not expect to be there. A recent survey
of Americans revealed that 90% of them expect to go to heaven. I
wish that was true but according to scripture there are going to be a
lot of surprised people.

Hell, according to Matthew chapter 25 was prepared not for
people but for the devil and his angels. But there isn't another
choice. When someone dies who is not right with God, there is
no other place for them to go. In Matthew 25:46 Jesus said, *"And
these will go into everlasting punishment, but the righteous will go into
everlasting life."*

In one verse Jesus refers to everlasting punishment and everlasting life. There is a heresy called universalism that first appeared
in the 3rd century which teaches that hell is temporary. It claims
that hell is not eternal punishment but temporary purification. This
heresy has regained some popularity lately. I wish that it was right.
However the problem is it isn't Biblical. Jesus describes both heaven
and hell with the same term. You can't have a temporary hell and an
eternal heaven.

Psalms 9:17 says, *"The wicked shall be turned into hell, And all
the nations that forget God."* It is a popular idea that only people like
Hitler, Stalin, and murderers go to hell. Notice this verse says that
"the nations that forget God" will be there as well. The sinner who
was given the death sentence and hung next to Jesus on the cross
repented and will be in heaven. There will be people in hell who
were never convicted of any crime. It is not about how big your sins
are, it is about whether you acknowledged God as your Savior. If you
"forget God" that is all it takes.

We learn a lot about what happens after death from the story
of Lazarus and the rich man. The Bible says of Lazarus that he dies
and angels carry him. Remember you are not a body. You live in a

body. You could call it your "earth suit" because, as long as you are in it you are here on earth, but when your body dies angels carry you. 2 Corinthians 5:8 says that *"to be absent from the body is to be present with the Lord."* Your body is only one part, according to 1 Thessalonians 5:23. You are three parts, it says; *"Now may the God of peace Himself sanctify you completely; and may your whole spirit, soul, and body be preserved blameless at the coming of our Lord Jesus Christ."*

This means no one stays behind to haunt a house. The house you live in isn't filled with the spirits of previous occupants. When those people died angels carried them away to either heaven or hell. I know there are stories of people communicating with the dead or other similar things. The Bible calls those "familiar spirits." That isn't someone's dead grandma. Their grandma is already gone. It is a demon spirit who may be familiar with grandma's life, but isn't grandma.

You have a spirit, which means you are immortal. God made you and so you have a beginning but you will not have an end. Just like angels cannot die, neither can your spirit. When God judges Satan and his angels, Jude 1:6 tells us they spend eternity in *"everlasting chains of darkness."* That is because as spirit beings they will never cease to exist, just like us. God breathed life into man. A dog or a squirrel is different from a man in that sense. God didn't make animals in His image to be spirit, soul, and body. Although we should still never be cruel to animals, animals are not equal people. And the life of a human is, therefore, always far more valuable.

Some more interesting things we learn from the account of Lazarus and the rich man is that we will recognize each other in heaven, we will remember our life on earth, and the relationships we made on earth will still be meaningful to us. The Bible tells us that the rich man recognized Lazarus a far off. He must have looked enough like himself to be recognized. Of course he would have been improved since he was no longer a beggar. But the rich man knew even a far off who he was. You will know people in heaven. In fact throughout the Bible a common phrase used to describe someone's death was "and they were gathered to their people." On earth there is a funeral where everyone sadly says good-bye, but in heaven the exact opposite is taking place. Loved ones are shouting for joy, thrilled to see their friends or family. The rich man was concerned for his family, asking Abraham to send them help. This shows us that our relationships will still be intact. If you care about someone on earth you will still care about them in heaven.

Most people who end up in hell will be surprised to be there. Notice that the rich man cried out to Abraham saying, *"Father Abraham, have mercy on me."* If the rich man, like the thief on the cross, had asked for mercy minutes or even seconds before death he would have received it. But once you die there is no more mercy to be had. This is clear in several places in scripture. Solomon refers to it in Ecclesiastes 11:3, *"Whether a tree falls to the south or to the north, in the place where it falls, there will it lie."* This isn't about lumber. He is saying that whatever state you are in when you die, that is how you will remain sealed for eternity. There will be no chance to rethink decisions, or undo mistakes. Ten seconds before death there is time, but after death there is not.

Let's look at Hebrews 12:14-16. *"Since the children have flesh and blood, He too shared in their humanity so that by His death He might destroy him who holds the power of death—that is, the devil—and free those who all their lives were held in slavery by their fear of death. For surely it is not angels He helps, but Abraham's descendants."* This is saying that you

YOU MUST STILL HAVE A FLESH AND BLOOD BODY TO EXPERIENCE FORGIVENESS OF SINS.

must still have a flesh and blood body to experience forgiveness of sins. Christ's death on the cross in a flesh and blood body made that possible. Christ's death was not helpful for the angels because they don't have a flesh and blood body. It was only the seed of Abraham who benefited. That is you and I. Revelations 20:10 says, *"The devil, who deceived them, was cast into the lake of fire and brimstone where the beast and the false prophet are. And they will be tormented day and night forever and ever.*" I think this is the scripture that the devil hates the most. I like to say, "If the devil tries to remind you of your past, you just remind him of his future."

In Jesus' day there were three groups of people. The Herodian's, who were pretty much political fanatics, there were the Pharisees who you probably remember were very legalistic, and there were the Sadducees. The Bible tells us about the Sadducees, that the Sadducees did not believe in angels or spirits and they did not believe in the resurrection from the dead. That is why the Sadducees were "Sad you see." If you didn't believe in any of those things you would be sad too. His response to them is recorded in Mathew 22:29-32. *'Jesus answered and said to them,'You are mistaken, not knowing the Scriptures nor the power of God. For in the resurrection they neither marry nor are given in marriage, but are like angels of God in heaven. But concerning the resurrection of the dead, have you not read what was spoken to you by God, saying, 'I am the God of Abraham, the God of Isaac, and the God of Jacob'? God is not the God of the dead, but of the living.'"* There is a resurrection of the just and the unjust. It is important that we do not behave as the Sadducees and hold tight to beliefs just because we like them. We must submit our theology to scripture and if scripture doesn't back it up, then throw it out.

Jesus spoke knowledgeably and authoritatively about the subjects of heaven and hell. Although we may not wish it to be true, hell is a real place. Here are some of the ways that scripture describes hell: Blackness and darkness, gnashing of teeth, unquenchable fire, a never dying worm, a place for unrepentant, perishing, burned but never exhausted, justice, suffering, torments, inescapable, separation from God, exclusion from heaven, regret, outer darkness, horror, eternal punishment, no rest day or night, bottomless pit, lake of fire, eternal second death, sorrow, remorse, and pain. Remember this is the Bible that said these things, not me. Hell is real. When faced with the reality of what hell is, we must not do nothing.

Charles Spurgeon lived from 1834 to 1892 and to this day he is referred to by many as the Prince of Preachers. He said this, "If sinners will be damned, at least let them leap to hell over our bodies, and if they perish, let them perish with our arms around their knees imploring them to stay. If hell must be filled, at least let it be filled in the teeth of our exertions, and let no one go there unwarned or unprayed for." I couldn't agree more.

Let's look at the heavenly side of eternity for a few moments. Ecclesiastes 3:11 says, *"God has set eternity in the hearts of men."* It doesn't matter if you go to the big cities in China and India, the jungles of the Amazon River in South America, or the savannas of Africa. No matter how far you search, people are worshipers. They worship God or worship something in His place. It is part of our very nature as humans. Those who claim not to worship usually worship themselves or each other. The greatest thing about heaven will be that God is there and we will worship Him. Philippians 3:20 says, *"Our citizenship is in heaven."* Our inheritance, too, is in heaven. Jesus said "I go to prepare a place for you and if I go to prepare a place for you I will come again." You and I are going to heaven if we have made Jesus Christ our Lord.

Did you realize that we will spend some time in heaven, but that we will spend most of eternity on earth? Revelation 21:1-2 says, *"Then I saw a new heaven and a new earth, for the first heaven and the first earth had passed away, and there was no longer any sea. I saw the Holy City, the new Jerusalem, coming down out of heaven from God, prepared as a bride beautifully dressed for her husband."*

In Genesis chapters 1 and 2 God creates this beautiful earth and a beautiful garden. He puts Adam and Eve in it and everything is magnificent. It has flowers, trees, mountains, streams; even God was pleased with the results. Then Satan comes with death sin, sickness, and disease. All of that continues until Revelation chapter 20:10 when Satan and his angels are thrown in the Lake of fire. The last two chapters of the Bible are like the first two. There is a restored earth. Paradise is regained. Revelation 21 actually tells us that God is going to come down out of heaven and live here with us.

This is part of why Christians should be environmentalists. Not the kind that view animal life as superior to human life but the kind who value the earth as a gift. Revelations actually says, "God will destroy those who destroy the earth."

When you and I travel we pack a suit case. When God travels He packs a city. Christians who have preceded us will be there. We can ask questions of our favorite people from the Bible.

I think some of the greatest things about heaven will be what isn't there. There will be no death, no rape, no ambulances, no aspirin, no pain, no sickness, no disease, no depression, no fear, no aging, no night, no sin, no missing children, no moth, no rust, no thieves, no abortion, no divorce court, no hard feelings, no bankruptcy, no psychiatric wards, no treatment centers, no pornography, no suicide, no aids, no cancer, no drug problems, no racial tension, no drive-by shootings, no accidents, no suffering, no locks, no sin, and of course no devil to resist.

The hope that we have, the hope that will not be cut off, is found in Jesus. He died on the cross and paid a debt that He did not owe, because you and I owed a debt we could not pay. Praise God for our blessed hope!

CHAPTER 27

YOU CAN'T KEEP A GOOD MAN DOWN "HOW TO GET UP WHEN YOU ARE DOWN"

"Do not lie in wait, O wicked man, against the dwelling of the righteous. Do not plunder his resting place. For a righteous man may fall seven times and rise again, but the wicked shall fall by calamity."

Proverbs 24:15-16

L et's also look at how this verse reads in the Message translation; *"Don't interfere with good people's lives; don't try to get the best of them. No matter how many times you trip them up, God-loyal people don't stay down long; soon they're up on their feet, while the wicked end up flat on their faces."*

Did you ever you get the idea that the righteous man just never makes mistakes? Did you ever think that really good Christians never fail? Or that pastors probably never sin anymore? Maybe you thought that your failures proved you were somehow unworthy to be a Christian? Solomon is telling us that the distinguishing feature of a "righteous" man or woman is not that they never fall, but that even

170

when they do, they get up again so quickly and so persistently that trying to keep them down is pointless. Have you ever tried to keep an inflated ball like a beach ball underwater? No matter how hard you push it down it will pop right back up, usually right in your face. That is a good

THE DISTINGUISHING FEATURE OF A "RIGHTEOUS" MAN OR WOMAN IS NOT THAT THEY NEVER FALL, BUT THAT EVEN WHEN THEY DO, THEY GET UP AGAIN

example of how the righteous man responds to difficulty or failure.

We are going to look at how a Christian should get up when knocked down. Someone said it this way. "When you have a set-back, don't take a step-back, because God has already prepared your comeback."

The Bible tells us that one of the names of Satan is "the accuser of the brethren." It is as if he sits on your shoulder saying, "Do it, do it, it is no big deal" and then the moment you do he switches to, "I can't believe you did that! You scum bag. I can't believe you call yourself a Christian. God is mad at you. He can't use you." It is important to realize where those thoughts come from and that they don't truly reflect God's view of us. To know what God thinks we must look at scripture.

1 John 1:9 says, *"If we confess our sins, He is faithful and just to forgive us of our sins and cleanse us from all unrighteousness."*

When God cleanses our sin it doesn't take him a week or even a day; He does it instantly. You may not feel forgiven, but that doesn't mean anything. I've had days when I didn't feel married, but that makes no difference; I still am. I remember being single and thinking that after the wedding I would "feel married." I got married, and to my surprise there wasn't a feeling that came with it. I was married, that was the truth. Goose bumps couldn't have made it any more real. If you asked God for forgiveness you received it. Whatever your expectations were, getting goose bumps won't change the fact that He forgives every time just as He promised. When God looks at you He sees Christ and He sees you perfect. That is where you are positionally. You are in Christ, a new creature. Old things have passed away, all things have become new. Experientially, God doesn't have any perfect people working for Him. Don't quit just because you feel like you failed.

The next time you think the devil is trying to condemn you, just remember this: Peter renounced the Lord, David committed adultery, Paul killed Christians, Jeremiah got depressed, Elijah ran in fear from Jezebel, Lot chose to live in Sodom, Abraham compromised with Hagar, and Isaac lied about his wife. Zechariah didn't believe the angel. Noah got drunk. Jacob lied. Joseph was spoiled. Moses stuttered. Gideon was afraid. Sampson was a womanizer. Rahab was a prostitute. David had an affair. Elijah was suicidal. Jonah ran from God. Naomi was a bitter widow. Job went bankrupt. The disciples fell asleep when they were supposed to be praying. Martha worried about everything. The Samaritan woman was divorced five times. Timothy had an ulcer. Thomas doubted Jesus, and John the Baptist ate bugs. But they all had something in common. God used each and every one of them.

God is a God of restoration. He will take things that you might believe are lost and restore them. He will turn the situation around. Often, we get so caught up in the moment that we believe that this must be the final nail in the coffin, it is the end.

I remember when Jeanie and I had been married less than a year. We had been missionaries for only a couple of months when we began to pastor a little church. The little church was growing and had about 120 people. However we had to renew the visas that gave us legal permission to be in Mexico. This meant driving back to the United States and then re-entering Mexico. To do this we were gone for ten days. During that short window of time a man from South America by the name of Lucio came into our church. He told our people that we were spies in the employ of the CIA. He made a long list of false and vicious claims against us. Not to mention he also taught heresy from our pulpit. The bottom line was that when we returned only ten days later he had already split the church.

I remember going house to house to talk to these people, many of whom we had stayed up late into the night counseling. People for whom we had made incredible sacrifices were slamming their doors in our faces. I remember one particular individual who spat in my face and called me an American demon and told me "get out of here in Jesus name." I went back to our vehicle, sat in the front seat, and cried like a baby. I said "God, I am the worst pastor in the world." At that moment I believed it. We hadn't been pastoring a year and already half of our people hated us. I felt like if anybody ever needed to leave the ministry it was me. But, fortunately, God wasn't as easily discouraged. I believe God likes to clean up messes. When He turns what looks like a hopeless cause into a success then He gets the glory.

David experienced a huge set back. In 1 Samuel chapter 30 the Bible says *"Now it happened, when David and his men came to Ziklag, on the third day, that the Amalekites had invaded the South and Ziklag, attacked Ziklag and burned it with fire, and had taken captive the women and those who were there, from small to great; they did not kill anyone, but carried them away and went their way. So David and his men came to the city, and there it was, burned with fire; and their wives, their sons, and their daughters had been taken captive. Then David and the people who were with him lifted up their voices and wept, until they had no more power to weep. And David's two wives, Ahinoam the Jezreelitess, and Abigail the widow of Nabal the Carmelite, had been taken captive. Now David was greatly distressed, for the people spoke of stoning him, because the soul of all the people was grieved, every man for his sons and his daughters. But David strengthened himself in the LORD his God."*

David's men were so distraught they considered stoning David. This is a great reminder that the throws of grief or depression are not the time to be making radical decisions. Stoning David would have solved nothing. In fact it would have made things worse. As a pastor I have witnessed countless times when people have made an emotional decision to quit, and immediately burned bridges. I have seen business men quit and pastors give their resignation and leave the ministry. Usually within a week, but nearly always within a month they say, "I can't believe I did that. That was stupid. I wish I could take it back." If you make decisions when you are depressed, almost always

THE THROWS OF GRIEF OR DEPRESSION ARE NOT THE TIME TO BE MAKING RADICAL DECISIONS.

it is the wrong decision. These men were on the verge of making one of those incredibly stupid decisions. But David, the Bible says, "encouraged himself in the Lord." It is great when your friends encourage you but sometimes none of them will. And then you have to do it yourself. This is a skill we should all work to develop. You have to get in the Word and remind yourself how much bigger God is than your situation. David did that. He left the place where he saw himself as nothing but a victim. That is a very dangerous place to be in, because, as long as you consider yourself a victim, nothing is going to change. It is your ex's fault, your parent's fault, your bosses' fault, society's fault, anyone's but your fault. Remember, God didn't make you a victim He made you a victor.

Encouraging yourself in God's Word or building yourself up in the faith is an important skill for a Christian. Jude 1:20-21 says, *"But you, Beloved, building yourselves up on your most holy faith, praying in the Holy Spirit, keep yourselves in the love of God, looking for the mercy of our Lord Jesus Christ unto eternal life."*

We need to turn to God and say, "What is my next step?" Psalms 37:23-24 says, *"The steps of a good man are ordered by the LORD, And He delights in his way. Though he fall, he shall not be utterly cast down; For the LORD upholds him with His hand.*

Here are some keys to getting up when you are knocked down:

#1 If it involves sin, repent.

1 John 1:8-9 says, *"If we say that we have no sin we deceive ourselves, and the truth is not in us. If we confess our sins, He is faithful and just to forgive us our sins and to cleanse us from all unrighteousness."* When you repent you aren't admitting something to God He didn't already know. You are choosing to reject instead of embrace that behavior. You are receiving forgiveness and committing to put up a fight if the behavior even thinks of returning.

#2 Look ahead. Focus on the future instead of the past.

David inquired of the Lord. He remembered that he had been called to be king. He knew there was a future in front of him. Philippians 2:13 says, *"For God Himself is at work in you, inspiring you to want the things that please him and to work for them."* (TNT) Did you realize that it is God who puts the desire in your heart, the dream, the picture, the hope, the future that you envision on the inside? We see a wonderful example in Acts 7:23 which says, *"And it came into the heart of Moses when he was a full 40 years old to go and visit the children of Israel."* God put that desire in his heart. It wasn't just random neurons firing.

When you are down, you need to look up and look forward. Don't look at your present situation or the past. You need a picture of where God is taking you in the future. That inspiration will pull you out of depression. Don't let your past dictate your future. Paul said it this way in Philippians 3:13, *"Brethren, I do not count myself to have apprehended; but one thing I do, forgetting those things which are behind and reaching forward to those things which are ahead."*

Israel gave us another very clear example of this. God told Jeremiah to prophesy to the people that if they did not repent the King of Babylon would come and take them captive. They didn't repent, and just as God had said the Babylonians came. Psalms 137 is written about their time in captivity. Listen to how it begins.

"By the rivers of Babylon, there we sat down. Yea, we wept when we remembered Zion. We hung our harps upon the willows in the midst of it. For there, those who carried us away captive asked of us a song, and

those who plundered us requested mirth, saying, 'Sing us one of the songs of Zion!' How shall we sing the Lord's song in a foreign land?"

Jeremiah was still prophesying after the defeat came that he had prophesied. Now he was telling them, "God has not forsaken you. Go to Babylon, build houses, plant vineyards, have your sons and daughters get married, pray for the peace of the city. Because as it prospers you are going to prosper and in 70 years, God is going to take you out of Babylon and bring you back to Jerusalem."

The Israelites had a word from God telling them not to mourn their loss or pine about what they didn't have. He told them to enjoy life, make the best of the situation. And then God promised them that they could be blessed in Babylon and that after a set time He would deliver them. They could have latched on to those promises and found hope. Instead they chose to look backwards at what could have been and they felt should have been and might have been. They had a pity party. The Bible says, *"They hung their harps in the willows."* The harp was the main instrument used in worship. They were basically saying "that they were so depressed they didn't even want to go to church and worship." Have you ever felt that way? So depressed you don't want to be at church. Perhaps someone drags you there and you see someone worshiping near you and you think "Hypocrite. I am sure they are messed up and just not admitting it." The reason the Israelites felt that way is the same reason that we sometimes do. They were focusing on the past, on what should have, could have, and might have been.

Our thoughts will very easily wander to the past and what could have been. But remember, our thoughts do not control us. We control our thoughts. Philippians 4:8 tells us how to think. It says, *"Finally brethren whatever things are true, whatever things are noble, whatever things are just, whatever things are pure, whatever things are holy. Whatever things leave a good rapport, if there is any virtue or anything praiseworthy, think on these things."*

#3 Forgive.

One of the reasons many people struggle to let go of their thoughts of the past is unforgiveness. Holding unforgiveness is like trying to drive forward while only looking in the rear view mirror. Most people who won't forgive feel as though they are hurting the person they won't forgive. However, when we forgive others it is really us who receive the gift of freedom. Bitterness is like drinking poison and then waiting for the other person to die. They won't die, you will. It is you who is drinking poison.

Many people have been genuinely hurt. They haven't forgiven and so it has become a broken heart. This doesn't just affect their relationship with the person who hurt them. It will affect all of their relationships. In fact, it can even affect their health. Proverbs 18:14 says, *"The spirit of a man will sustain him in sickness, but who can bear a broken spirit."* Doctors may not be able to fully explain it but if you ask them they have probably noticed this principle in action. This verse is telling us that if your spirit is strong and healthy it can sustain even your physical body during sickness. But when your spirit is broken and wounded, and adversity comes, you will fall. A more well-known scripture that refers to this is Proverbs 17:22 which says *"A merry heart does good, like medicine, But a broken spirit dries the bones."* It is scripturally very clear that your attitude, the condition of your spirit, will significantly affect your ability to handle difficulty. Don't let unforgiveness hold you down. As Ephesians 4:6 says *"Be angry, and do not sin; do not let the sun go down on your wrath."* Picture someone being knocked down while wearing a 200 lb. back pack. Then imagine that they try to stand back up without taking it off. That is like trying to get up while carrying unforgiveness.

Hebrews 12:15-16 says, *"Looking carefully lest anyone fall short of the grace of God; lest any root of bitterness springing up cause trouble, and by this many become defiled; lest there be any fornicator or profane person like Esau, who for one morsel of food sold his birthright."* Did you notice that Paul connected Esau's loss of his birth right to bitterness? A Jewish Rabbi explains, "Esau had a very busy day. Among other things he had murdered a man and stolen his wife. This brief mention of Esau's adultery is not incidental but central to the plot." It is truly foolish of us to think that we can contain bitterness. It cannot be focused like a laser; it is more like an atom bomb causing damage in every direction.

So, if there is unforgiveness in your life, call the bomb squad! Get rid of it. Mark 11:25-26 says, *"And whenever you stand praying, if you have anything against anyone, forgive him, that your Father in heaven may also forgive you your trespasses. But if you do not forgive, neither will your Father in heaven forgive your trespasses."*

Two things in this verse stand out to me. First, that forgiveness is something you can do "whenever you pray." It doesn't take months. It is a decision you make and reaffirm at least as often as you pray, which should be very often. Secondly, that the forgiveness you receive is connected to the forgiveness you give. That by itself should be all the reason we need to be the most forgiving people who ever lived.

#4 Speak God's will into the situations.

Jesus told us to pray, *"Your will be done on earth as it is it heaven."* The reason He said this was because God's will isn't always done on earth. Some people believe that absolutely everything that happens is God's will. That idea "everything that happens is the inevitable will of God" is Buddhism. That is Hinduism. That is not Christianity. People slip into eternity every day without God and we know according to Timothy that *"God wills that all men be saved and come to the knowledge of the truth."*

Proverbs 15:23 says, *"A man has joy by the answer of his mouth, and a word spoken in due season, how good it is!"* Over 90% of people believe that joy comes because your circumstances look good. That isn't Biblical, which is another way of saying it isn't true. The truth is that you have joy because of your words. We need to realize that we can have peace, deliverance, healing, and victory as a result of "the answer of our mouths."

#5 Recall God's Goodness.

Psalms 116:7 says, *"Return to your rest, oh my soul, for the Lord has dealt bountifully with you."* In one of David's most difficult times, as he was feeling discouraged, he began to recount what God had done for him. In verse 8 he says, *"For you delivered my soul from death."* For 13 years Saul tried to kill David; twice Saul threw a spear at him. David continues, "and my eyes from tears." David made some bad choices, and as a result there were some very devastating things took place in his home. One of his sons murdered his own brother. One of David's own sons tried to kill David. He had a young child born in his house that died. There were many bad things that happened in David's life. Yet David said, "You delivered my eyes from tears." He is saying that despite the things that happened, God healed his broken heart. David also says, "My feet from falling." Remember that David committed adultery and then murdered the woman's husband by having his troops retreat from him when he was in battle. In spite of that David repented and God forgave him. David says "You have taken my feet out of the miry clay. You have set me on a solid rock and you have put me in a large place." David is recalling how God saved him from his own sinful deeds. As he begins to rehearse what God had done for him his heart begins to rise.

David had enough difficulty in life that he could have made a full time job of dwelling on it. However when he remembered his past he focused on how God had rescued him from his trouble. Many people would have dwelled on the trouble itself. David knew better. This is something we all need to learn.

Peter learned it. He had renounced Christ on the night before he was killed. But by the time Pentecost came about 50 days later, Peter wasn't focused on his failure anymore. He had accepted forgiveness. He knew it didn't matter anymore. Just like 2 Corinthians 5:17 tells us, *"Therefore, if anyone is in Christ, he is a new creation; old things have passed away; behold, all things have become new."*

CHAPTER 28

VENGEANCE IS MINE

"Do not rejoice when your enemy falls, and do not let your heart be glad when he stumbles; Lest the LORD see it, and it displease Him, And He turn away His wrath from him."

Proverbs 24:17-18

When someone does you wrong, no matter how obvious their motives seem to be, remember that we really don't know everything about the situation. We don't know their full intentions or their motives. We can't even know all of the facts. We often think that we know what happened, but in reality only God knows the situation fully. God says, "leave the vengeance to me." He reserves the right to exact payment, vengeance, and judgment for every wrong committed.

Hebrews 10:30 says, *"For we know Him Who said, "Vengeance is Mine, I will repay,"* says the Lord. And again, *"The LORD will judge His people."* In Deuteronomy 32:35 it says nearly the same thing again. *"Vengeance is Mine, and recompense; their foot shall slip in due time; for the day of their calamity is at hand, and the things to come hasten upon them."* This verse is saying that vengeance *"hastens upon them."* In other words it may not come every Friday, but vengeance is definitely coming. It is important to realize that God is always just.

However, He is not usually in the same hurry to pass judgment that we are. The Bible shows us that God delights in mercy. I think one of the greatest examples of God's patience to judge is found in Genesis chapter 5. Enoch was the 7th from Adam. Enoch appears several places in your Bible. He is quoted in the New Testament and he prophesies about the Day of Judgment, when Jesus returns with his saints to execute judgment on the ungodly. Enoch also prophetically saw the judgment that was going to take place on the earth in the days of Noah. In fact, when his child was born, God said to Enoch, "When this boy dies, I will judge the earth." So Enoch named his son Methuselah, which means, "At your death judgment falls."

How would you like a name like that? Perhaps it made people think twice if they considered doing him harm. The interesting thing about Methuselah is how long he lived. God had promised to judge the earth at Methuselah's death. It seems that for that reason God kept Methuselah living. At 900 years old God wanted to give people more time to repent. At 950 God still wanted to give people more time. Genesis 5:27 tells us that Methuselah lived to be 969 years old! He became the oldest person to ever live. It wasn't because he watched his cholesterol so closely. It was because God kept extending mercy to the people of the world. God continues to do that today. Sometimes people see the mercy of God and think that He is passing over their sin. They seem to believe that God is winking at what they have done. That is not the case at all. He is just being merciful.

In a previous chapter we discussed adversity and how the presence of adversity doesn't automatically mean you did something wrong. The flip side is also true. The absence of judgment doesn't automatically mean that everything that has been done has been acceptable to God. It could be that judgment is simply delayed. God's Word is His standard of right and wrong. No one has VIP sinning privileges. Perhaps that seems funny. But I have talked with people who claimed that very thing. People in adulterous relationships who convince themselves that God made an exception because this was their soul mate. Christians, even ministers, who believed that because God still used them He must be accepting of the sin in some corner of their life. These people mistook mercy for acceptance. Because no lightning bolts appeared the moment they sinned they assume God has given them a sin for free card. They act as if they don't need to repent of their sin because they don't see the judgment. Those people are wrong.

Romans 12:19 says, *"Beloved, do not avenge yourselves, but rather give place to wrath; for it is written, "Vengeance is Mine, I will repay," says the Lord."*

Notice that if you avenge yourself then God does not avenge you. The scripture continues in verse 20 saying, *"Therefore if your enemy is hungry, feed him; If he is thirsty, give him a drink; for in so doing you will heap coals of fire on his head."*

The Bible is telling us that when someone treats you wrong, instead of retaliating, you should respond with kindness. This is the exact opposite of what your flesh would like to do. The Bible says, *"Those who lose their life will find it. Those who give will receive. And if someone slaps you, you should turn the other cheek."* It may not seem natural, but that is how to overcome evil.

Proverbs 11:31 says, *"If the righteous will be recompensed on the earth, how much more the ungodly and the sinner."* The Bible is telling us that not only is a judgment day to come where everyone's accounts will be settled with God, but even on earth there is recompense. However, not everyone receives their judgment here on earth. For example with Hitler, Stalin, or the terrorists of 9/11, it's obvious that there needs to be more judgment. God says it is coming.

I Timothy 5:24 says, *"Some men's sins are clearly evident, preceding them to judgment, but those of some men follow later."* Sometimes we clearly see people's sin and we may even be able to observe as they receive judgment for that sin here on earth. The Bible is clear, however, that sometimes we won't be able to observe justice. In those cases it is a mistake to assume that justice is therefore not served. What matters isn't whether or not we see it. It matters that God is the righteous Judge.

David and Bathsheba are powerful examples. Most of us remember the story of how David was the king of Israel. He walks out on the roof of the palace. As David looks over the walls and fences of the neighboring homes he sees Bathsheba, who is bathing at her home. David sends for her, he seduces her, and they commit adultery. Bathsheba's husband is away serving in David's military. When David discovers that Bathsheba is pregnant he tries to have Uriah, Bathsheba's husband, brought back in time for Uriah to believe himself the father but the plan fails. So David sends orders to attack a strong city. He specifies that Uriah is to lead the attack and that the army is to withdraw from him so he will be killed. David's plan succeeds and Uriah is killed in battle. David then takes Bathsheba as his own wife.

For a short while it appears that David has gotten away with adultery and murder. Then the prophet Nathan comes to David and confronts him for his sin. Some of Nathan's words are found in 2 Samuel 12:9-14. *"Why have you despised the commandment of the LORD, to do evil in His sight? You have killed Uriah the Hittite with the sword; you have taken his wife to be your wife, and have killed him with the sword of the people of Ammon. Now therefore, the sword shall never depart from your house, because you have despised Me, and have taken the wife of Uriah the Hittite to be your wife.' Thus says the LORD: 'Behold, I will raise up adversity against you from your own house; and I will take your wives before your eyes and give them to your neighbor, and he shall lie with your wives in the sight of this sun. For you did it secretly, but I will do this thing before all Israel, before the sun.'"* So David said to Nathan, *"I have sinned against the LORD."* And Nathan said to David, *"The LORD also has put away your sin; you shall not die. However, because by this deed you have given great occasion to the enemies of the LORD to blaspheme, the child also who is born to you shall surely die."*

I want you to see that David repented and God forgave him, but there were still consequences for his actions. It is like a depressed and suicidal person jumping from a 60 story building. As they pass the 40th story they cry out to God and say, "I am sorry, please forgive me." Does God hear them? Yes. Does he forgive them? Yes. Is gravity still pulling them down? Unfortunately yes. Their guilt is gone but the consequences of their previous decision to jump are still fast approaching.

Nathan actually details to David what some of the consequences will be. He said that the child would die. He said that an adversary would rise up from within his own house. That turned out to be Absalom, who began by killing his own brother, Amnon. Then he led a rebellion against David. He slept with David's wives, in the open just as Nathan had prophesied. Absalom instigated a war in which he died along with 20,000 other men. Then Adonijah, another of David's sons,

MANY PEOPLE BELIEVE THAT FORGIVENESS MEANS THAT ALL CONSEQUENCES ARE IMMEDIATELY CANCELED. DAVID IS PROOF THAT ISN'T THE CASE.

also rebelled against David and the rebellion was put down. However, Solomon eventually had to have Adonijah killed because he attempted yet another rebellion. Was David forgiven? Yes he was. But were there consequences for his actions? Yes there were. The difference here is we have Nathan's prophecy to help us recognize the connection between David's sin and these actions. Most of the time when justice is served there is no prophecy to explain the connection. Many people believe that forgiveness means that all consequences are immediately canceled. David is proof that isn't the case.

There is coming a day of judgment. In fact Isaiah 61:2 calls it *"the day of vengeance of our God."* Most often we hear it referred to just as "Judgment Day." Revelation chapter 20 describes it in detail starting in verse 11. *"Then I saw a great white throne* (this is referred to as the white throne judgment) *and Him who sat on it from whose face the earth and the heaven fled away. And there was found no place for them. And I saw the dead, small and great, standing before God, and books were opened. And another book was opened, which is the Book of Life."*

On one side there is just one book, the Book of Life. And on the other side there are multiple books. Theologians usually call these the Books of Works because the verse continues and says, *"And the dead were judged according to their works, by the things which were written in the books. The sea gave up the dead who were in it, and Death and Hades delivered up the dead who were in them. And they were judged, each one according to his works. Then Death and Hades were cast into the lake of fire. This is the second death. And anyone not found written in the Book of Life was cast into the lake of fire."*

It is important to notice that the Books of Works are not the criteria by which anyone is cast into the lake of fire. That is decided by the presence of their name in the Book of Life. That is where the names of all who have received Jesus as Lord of their life are written. It is not our works that get us into heaven; it is Jesus' finished work.

Many Christians imagine that heaven is like what communism tried to be, a place where everyone receives the exact same thing regardless of their actions. It is true that salvation is not earned. However the Bible is very clear that there are rewards that are based on our works. Heaven will not be identical experiences for everyone. Jesus discusses that in Revelation 3:11. He says, *"Hold fast to what you have. Let no one take your crown."* There are rewards coming, and there are things you can do that would cause your reward to be lost or "taken." A deeper study of all that will be for another book and another day.

No work, good or bad, is going to go unnoticed or unaddressed by God. 1 Peter 3:9 says, *"The Lord is not slack concerning His promises, as some count slackness, but long suffering towards us, not willing that any should perish, but that all should come to repentance."* We can truly rest in the knowledge that God will handle any situation where we feel a need for vengeance.

What if, however, someone has done you a great wrong? Jesus answers this question in Mark 11:25. He says, *"And whenever you stand praying, if you have anything against anyone, forgive him that your Father in heaven may also forgive you your trespasses."* Forgiveness is letting go of your perceived right to exact punishment or seek vengeance. It is not saying that what they did was right. It is not even saying that you will pretend it never happened. It doesn't mean you immediately trust them again. Joseph was beat up, thrown into a pit, and then sold into slavery by his jealous brothers. Seventeen years later when he met them again in Egypt he had forgiven them but he didn't trust them right away. He took some time to test their character to discover if they had changed.

If a friend or family member stole your wallet and maxed out your credit cards, you need to forgive them. But, if a week later they ask to take your credit card to the store to buy you a coke, it is ok to send them with a five dollar bill instead of your credit card. Even though you forgave them it may take time before you trust them. Jesus said in Matthew 3:8, *"Therefore bear fruits worthy of repentance."* Trust will come with time as they bear fruit that shows their repentance.

It is important that we recognize how dangerous it is to latch on to vengeance ourselves. Bitterness can affect us in so many ways. Ahithophel was one of David's counselors. Scripture actually tells us that he was very wise. It says in 2 Samuel 16:23, *"Now the advice of Ahithophel, which he gave in those days, was as if one had inquired at the oracle of God."* That is a serious compliment. Ahithophel had a problem though. He had a granddaughter named Bathsheba. King David seduced her, and had his son in law killed. Ahithophel never forgave David for what he did. That bitterness grew in him. And although he had great wisdom his bitterness caused him to not apply wisdom in his own life. Ahithophel allowed the worst in David to bring out the worst in himself. He allowed the carnality in David to bring out the carnality in himself. And it literally destroyed Ahithophel's life. Ahithophel joined Absalom's rebellion, which failed. Ahithophel lost his title, his position, his influence, and his life.

In the book of Ruth we find the story of Haman. He was prime minister of Persia. Persia had 128 states. It was the most powerful empire the world had ever seen up until that time. As prime minister he was the second most powerful man alive. He was also most likely the second richest. He had 12 sons, and everything that money could buy including fame, influence, and power.

AHITHOPHEL ALLOWED THE WORST IN DAVID TO BRING OUT THE WORST IN HIMSELF.

But he hated a Jew by the name of Mordecai. Haman was so bitter with Mordecai that not only did he want to kill Mordecai but he decided to kill Mordecai along with as many Jews as possible. He constructed special gallows where he planned to watch Mordecai die.

At a party with his family and friends Haman is supposed to be rejoicing over a recent promotion. He lists his riches and his accomplishments and then says, "And none of this means anything to me as long as I see Mordecai the Jew sitting in the King's gate." What he was saying is, "Although I have a great life, I don't enjoy it." When we allow bitterness into our lives, when we seek vengeance on our own, it poisons our insides. You can have a great family, but you won't appreciate them. You can have a great job, but won't appreciate it. A great car, plenty of food, clothes, everything you need, but none of it will satisfy you when there is bitterness and vengeance in your heart. God says leave the vengeance to Him. Not so He can save that person from what you might do to them, but so he can save you from what bitterness will do to you.

You will be mistreated, probably even this week. But I urge you follow the godly advice Solomon is giving us. Don't seek to avenge the wrong, just forgive. As Jesus said, each time you pray be sure you have forgiven everyone and you will walk free.

CHAPTER 29

THINK RIGHTEOUS THOUGHTS

"Don't bother your head with braggarts or wish you could succeed like the wicked. Those people have no future at all; they are headed down a dead end street."
Proverbs 24:19-20 (MSG)

The King James Version says it this way, *"Fret not thyself because of evil men, neither be thou envious at the wicked; for there shall be no reward to the evil man; the candle of the wicked shall be put out."*
Many of us at one time or another have observed the wicked and thought "Things seem so good for them. It seems like it would be nice to live like that. What would my life be like if I lived without moral constraints?" Solomon admits that thought even crossed his mind. But remember what Solomon told us in Proverbs 23:7, *"As a man thinks in his heart, so will he become."* Our thoughts precede our actions. Ultimately you are going to move in the direction of your thoughts. That is why 2 Corinthians 10:5 tells us to *"take every thought captive into the obedience of Christ."*
Even though this is a thought we should not welcome, it is a common one. David, who was Solomon's father, also asked himself

that question in Psalms 73:12-19. He says, *"This is what the wicked are like—always carefree, they increase in wealth. Surely in vain have I kept my heart pure; in vain have I washed my hands in innocence. All day long I have been plagued; I have been punished every morning. If I had said, "I will speak thus," I would have betrayed your children. When I tried to understand all this, it was oppressive to me till I entered the sanctuary of God; then I understood their final destiny. Surely you place them on slippery ground; you cast them down to ruin. How suddenly are they destroyed, completely swept away by terrors."*

David is being transparent. He allows us to follow him through his question, his frustration, and then to the answer. He begins like many of us who observe the success of the wicked and he admits that he feels he has "kept his heart pure in vain." His thoughts begin to stray from the present as he admits that if he had allowed his thoughts to become words and actions it would have

IT WAS NOT UNTIL HE BEGAN TO THINK BEYOND TODAY, THAT HE REALIZED HOW RIDICULOUS HE WAS TO FEEL JEALOUS

had consequences for his grandkids. David says it was not until he began to think beyond today, that he realized how ridiculous he was to feel jealous. When he considered the future that lay in store for the wicked, the fleeting success they currently enjoy is no longer attractive, when the future judgment for their actions gets included in the deal.

We need to be mindful of a truth that is easy to ignore. Jesus said in John 10:10 that, *"The thief comes to steal, kill and destroy."* There is a devil and according to 1 Peter 5:8 we should *"be self-controlled and alert. Your enemy the devil prowls around like a roaring lion looking for someone to devour."* If the wicked are already headed for destruction "on a dead end street" then why would Satan waste his energy on them?

Jesus said a very interesting thing in Mark chapter 4. This is where He tells the parable of the sower. He says the sower goes out and He sows the word of the kingdom. Let's look closely at verses 16 and 17. *"These likewise are the ones sown on stony ground who, when they hear the word, immediately receive it with gladness; and they have no root in themselves, and so endure only for a time. Afterward, when tribulation or persecution arises for the word's sake, immediately they stumble."* Jesus specifically said that when these hearts had gladly received God's word "for the word's sake" tribulations came. Jesus is telling us that being a Christian won't guarantee that life will be a bed of roses. In fact it will put a bull's eye on your back. There will be "tribulations" or difficulties that will come your way expressly because you have chosen to live by God's Word. If you have been hearing the word, if you've been studying the word, if you have been meditating on the word, Satan is going to try to use trials and tribulations to steal it from your heart. What are tribulations? It could be a layoff at work, or the car and the washing machine both breaking down. Anything the devil can use to get you to give up, he will. That is why the Bible tells us in Galatians 6:9 *"And let us not grow weary while doing good, for in due season we shall reap if we do not lose heart."* It may not be instantly but in "due season" righteousness will pay off.

David came to his epiphany in the "Sanctuary of God." Often the answer to our questions are found at church. There, David was reminded of eternity. It is amazing how we can move through life day after day, week after week, and just not think about eternity. It is easy to get caught up in the things of life and not give the future a thought. That is what the wicked are doing. They are walking with their head down unable to see the dangers they are headed straight for. Proverbs 14:12 says, *"There is a way that seems right to a man, but its end is the way of death."* In our 29th saying, at the end of verse 20, Solomon said, *"The candle of the wicked shall be put out."* He is reminding us that eternity is coming, and eternity matters. Wishing for something without considering its long term effects is not wise. But that is exactly what the devil hopes we will do.

I have good news for you. Satan hasn't changed his approach in 6000 years. The bad news is that people are still falling for the same tricks. In the Garden of Eden, when Satan set out to deceive Eve, he said, "Has God said you shall not eat of these trees?" and she said, "Yes we are not supposed to eat." Then Satan said, "You will not surely die." After all this time Satan is still doing the same thing. He wants you to question what God actually said. And if he can't convince you God never said it then he tries to convince you that somehow, for you, in these circumstances, it is not true, or doesn't apply. He will say things like these: "Well, that's true, but not for you." Or "it's not true for today." "It isn't true anymore." He will try to convince you that it isn't really wrong. His goal is get you to stray from God's Word. If he can get you to use anything but God's Word as your standard then he knows he can win. There are many standards to pick from. Culture, religion, logic, the laws of the land, even the best of these if followed long enough will allow you to stray from God's Word. For example, we cannot allow the law to be our standard of right and wrong. There are plenty of sins that are 100% legal. Porn and abortion for example are both very legal. But that doesn't make them ok in God's eyes. This may sound obvious but, George Barna of the Christian research organization says that only 10% of those who profess to be Christians have a Christian world view. In other words only 10% of Christians take their values, their morals, and their understandings straight from the Bible. The other 90% have fallen for Satan's trick. They are making their decisions and basing their values on something other than scripture.

The antidote for temptation and wrong thinking is God's Word. That is why when Jesus was tempted He answered, "It is written." The question this raises is, "Who is Lord of your life?" If we have made Jesus the Lord of our lives then it is His Word that should establish our values, our morals. It is His Word that should direct our decisions.

You must recognize that God's Word is speaking to you. It reveals God's will for your life. Maybe my wife is about to go to the store and I tell her, "Please remember to get my favorite cheese." She has now been made aware of my will. Likewise God has revealed His will for us in the Bible. Our choice is what we do with what we know is His will. As a Christian, the Bible should be the first place that you turn for answers. Don't fall for Satan's tricks, there is no other standard. God's Word is it!

Psalms 19:7-11 says, *"The law of the LORD is perfect, converting the soul; The testimony of the LORD is sure, making wise the simple; The statutes of the LORD are right, rejoicing the heart; The commandment of the LORD is pure, enlightening the eyes; The fear of the LORD is clean, enduring forever; The judgments of the LORD are true and righteous altogether. More to be desired are they than gold, Yea, than much fine gold; Sweeter also than honey and the honeycomb. Moreover by them your servant is warned, and in keeping them there is great reward."*

Hebrews 11:6 says, *"But without faith it is impossible to please Him, for he who comes to God must believe that He is, and that He is a rewarder of those who diligently seek Him."*

Scripture is clear that in order to please God we must first know that God exists. The very next thing we need is to understand that God is a rewarder. We need not doubt if living righteously is worthwhile. God promises us it is.

CHAPTER 30

SUBMIT TO AUTHORITY

"My son, fear the LORD and the king; do not associate with those given to change; for their calamity will rise suddenly, and who knows the ruin those two can bring?"
Proverbs 24:21-22

I want to focus on two things that this last saying can teach us. The first is to submit to authority. It says, "Fear the Lord and fear the King." Rebellion is an ungodly thing. The original rebel is none other than Satan himself. In our culture it is easy to forget that God is displeased by rebellion. In our movies the hero is almost always rebellious. He is breaking rules and the audience is expected to like him for it. Our culture glorifies rebellion. The Bible does not. In fact it says in 1 Samuel 15:23, *"For rebellion is as the sin of witchcraft."* Considering whom the original rebel is it shouldn't be such a surprise. Rebellion is demonic. That is why in 1 Corinthians chapter 11 it says, *"A woman should have a sign of authority on her head because of the angels."* I remember years ago in Bible school, we didn't have a clue what that meant. And every time we didn't understand a

OUR CULTURE GLORIFIES REBELLION. THE BIBLE DOES NOT.

scripture we would half-jokingly say, "It must be because of the angels." Years later while serving as a missionary I began to understand.

For two years my wife and I lived and worked with the Otomi Indians of Central Mexico. They had a similar custom as the one discussed in that verse in Corinthians. The married women wore shawls or something resembling a lace doily on their heads as a symbol of their submission to their husbands and to God. I remember visiting the home of a pastor after a meeting to have the typical beans, rice, tortillas, and coffee. I almost hesitate to call it just coffee, because it was what they call "cafe con leche." It is about 1/3 coffee 1/3 milk and seemingly 1/3 sugar. As we arrived and began receiving our "cafe con leche" it became obvious that one of the couples present were having an argument. I don't know what the husband said to his wife, but whatever it was it really upset her. She stood up as tall as she could which was probably, only about 4 foot 8 inches. She grabbed the covering on her head, yanked it off, and threw it on the floor. She then proceeded to shout at him in the Otomi language. Because I could only speak with them in Spanish, to this day I don't have a clue what she said. But thanks to her head covering I know pretty well the nature of her statements. At the end of her brief tirade she stopped shouting. She meekly replaced her head covering and then went to a far corner of the room where she knelt and began to pray. That shawl represented her submission. When for that brief moment she could not restrain herself enough to submit she took it off. In her culture it was meaningful. In our culture it isn't. We rely more on the display of our attitude than we do on a head covering. At the end of that chapter Paul says, "If anyone is contentious, we have no such custom, nor do the churches of God." So we realize a head covering is something to do with that culture, and not a biblical necessity but, the principle is still the same. For example, a married business man or woman who removes their wedding ring for the purpose of being able to more freely get flirtatious attention from strangers when they travel is doing something very wrong. It is not wrong because having an empty ring finger is sin. It is wrong because removing something that is a meaningful sign of your commitment and mutual submission is a sinful act of the heart.

Why do the angels benefit from seeing that we take submission seriously? Consider what they have witnessed. Satan, who must be quite a salesman, convinced 1/3 of the angels to rebel with him against God. The angels saw the fruit of rebellion; they saw the results of the rebellion of Satan and his angels. Angels do not like rebellion. It is good to remember also that angels surround us even now. God and angels both are offended by rebellion.

Rebellion is an attack or disregard of authority and there are three areas of authority. There is divine authority, there is governmental authority, and there is what we will call family authority.

Because rebellion is a spiritual and demonic thing there is no such thing as rebellion in only one area. You can't rebel against your parents while remaining in submission to God and the civil authorities in your life. It doesn't work that way. When you rebel in one area you are rebelling to at least a degree in all of the areas. Remember, rebellion is very dangerous stuff. Don't allow our culture to convince you to treat it as a virtue. God's standard is what matters and He says it is like witchcraft.

The second point I want to touch on that Solomon brings up in the last of his 30 sayings is about change. He said, "Do not associate with those who are given to change. For their calamity will rise suddenly." What is Solomon talking about? Is he saying that we should avoid people who change at all? Since he just finished giving us 29 ways in which we can change for the better it is pretty safe to assume that he doesn't mean that we should not grow and change for the better. What Solomon is talking about when he says "given to change" is the person who is perpetually flip-flopping and changing everything. Someone who can't commit to a thing long enough to see it through.

As a pastor and former missionary I have served on several different missions boards. On one board I met someone who I believe is

a good example of what Solomon is talking about. He was the direc-
tor of a particular missions organization. He would start by telling
us how God was leading the organization to get involved in West
India. A month later with equal passion he would say, "No, now it
is East India." Another short while later he would say "No, now
God has called this organization to focus on Africa." Predictably
the calling to Africa was replaced in short order with a passionate
declaration that the organization was being called to focus on Haiti.
On and on it would go. How can anyone follow this? Every time you
turned around there was another radical change. This sort of insta-
bility, Solomon says, don't associate with.

To bring growth and change to your life is good. The Bible tells
us you are to be changed from glory to glory and from faith to faith.
So there has to be change, and there is such a thing as good change.
But constant radical change is dangerous.

I believe there are few better examples in our time of consis-
tency and healthy change than Billy Graham. He is nearing 100
years of age. That is a long time to be doing the same thing. He has
been incredibly consistent. We might say that he started out saying
"you must be born again" and then he switched to "you must be born
from above." But what he meant by it never changed. For almost
80 years of ministry he has been calling people to repentance. It is
interesting that after all these years there is low turnover on his staff
and board. Many have come this whole way with him.

In the 1990's after over 50 years in the ministry, Billy Graham
decided he was going to do "youth services." He was seventy years
old and he wanted to do youth events. For all those years he had
always worn a suit. He got rid of the suit. He always had the same
kind of music. He brought in very popular Christian artists and
found young Christian athletes who would testify. Guess what
happened? At his first youth event he had 65,000 people attend!
He tried something new, but something that didn't change was his
message. He changed his method but not his message. His vision
stayed the same.

It is human nature that we form attachments to things and routines. For example you probably sit at the same place at your dining room table. And you probably sleep on the same side of the bed each night. As a Pastor, I know that most of my congregation sits in almost the same spot every week. Even though there are thousands of people, if I want to find someone while I am preaching I usually can by just looking in the vicinity of "their pew." We often put a high value on stability, and predictability. It is important to remember that, although the message of the Gospel is timeless and unchanging, the method is not sacred. Hebrews 13:8 says, *"Jesus is the same yesterday, today and forever."* He is perfect and unchanging. You and I however have a long way to go. Romans 8 says, *"We are predestined to be conformed to the image of His Son."* I know I am not a perfect reflection of Jesus yet, and I believe I can safely say neither are you. There will be change in our life as we conform to His image.

On the other hand there are people, organizations, or churches that are constantly making radical changes. Those whose vision seems to switch every time you turn to look. These we must avoid.

George Barna, in his book "The Boiling Point," has some powerful observations about the change, both good and bad, our culture has endured. He said:

> "We have taller buildings and shorter tempers. Wider freeways and narrower viewpoints. We spend more and have less. We buy more and enjoy less. We have bigger houses and smaller families. More conveniences but less time. We have more degrees and less sense, more knowledge and less judgment, more experts but more problems. We have more medicine but less wellness. We drink too much, smoke too much, spend too recklessly, drive too fast, get too angry too quickly, stay up too late, get up too tired, read too seldom, watch TV too much, and we pray too little. We have multiplied our possessions and reduced our value. We talk too much, love too seldom, and hate too often. We've

learned how to make a living but not a life. We've added years to our life but not life to our years. We've been all the way to the moon and back but have trouble crossing the street to meet a new neighbor; we've conquered outer space but not our inner space. We've done many larger things but often not better things. We split the atom but not our prejudice. We write more and learn less. We plan more and accomplish less. We've learned to rush but not to wait. We build more computers to hold more information to produce more copies than ever and have less real communication. These are the times of fast food and slow digestion, tall men with short character, steep profits and shallow relationships. These are times of world peace but domestic warfare, more leisure but less fun, more kinds of food and less nutrition. These are the days of two incomes but more divorces. Fancier houses but broken homes. These are the days of quick trips, disposable diapers, and throw away morality."

As we finish the 30 sayings of Solomon, I find it very appropriate that we finish discussing the pros and cons of change. Solomon has given us a wide variety of advice. He has shown us how to choose friends, and how to be better children and parents. He talked about money and debt. We looked at our homes and our businesses. We looked at the present as well as eternity. We have learned about our emotions as well as our words. We talked about helping others and seeking help ourselves. So many topics in such a short time.

Now it is time to make changes in our own lives. I encourage you to ask God for the wisdom to select what areas He would have you focus on. Make those changes endure. It is my prayer that this book will not just tickle your ears but instead it will inspire your heart. Also, that if anyone has read this book before making God the source of all wisdom, the Lord of their life, that somehow this book, by inspiration of the Holy Spirit, will inspire you to take that step. That is the most crucial change of all.

If you have accepted Jesus as Lord of your life, if you have accepted his forgiveness of your sin, then you are right with God. You know beyond a shadow of a doubt that if your heart stopped today and you faced eternity you would spend eternity with God.

IF YOU ARE NOT RIGHT WITH GOD THERE IS NO NEED TO PUT IT OFF EVEN ONE MORE DAY

However, if you are not right with God there is no need to put it off even one more day. Romans 10:9 says, *"If you confess with your mouth the Lord Jesus and believe in your heart that God has raised Him from the dead, you will be saved."* If you wonder what you need to be saved from, the answer is that we all need to be saved from the sin that separates us from God. I invite you to do precisely what that verse says. Pray the following prayer and God Himself has promised that He will forgive your sin, and make you a new person on the inside.

"Dear God, I believe that You sent Jesus Who lived a sinless life and then suffered death on the cross, not for His sin but for mine. I believe that on the third day Jesus rose from the dead. I accept the forgiveness You freely offer. I pledge to make You Lord of my life and to seek to please You. I thank You for Your love and forgiveness. In Jesus' name, Amen."